Story Power!

Breathing Life into History

Story Power!

Breathing Life into History

Elizabeth Cervini Manvell

ROWMAN & LITTLEFIELD EDUCATION

A division of

ROWMAN & LITTLEFIELD PUBLISHERS, INC.
Lanham • New York • Toronto • Plymouth, UK

Published by Rowman & Littlefield Education
A division of Rowman & Littlefield Publishers, Inc.
A wholly owned subsidiary of The Rowman & Littlefield Publishing Group, Inc.
4501 Forbes Boulevard, Suite 200, Lanham, Maryland 20706
http://www.rowmaneducation.com

Estover Road, Plymouth PL6 7PY, United Kingdom

Copyright © 2011 by Elizabeth Cervini Manvell

All rights reserved. No part of this book may be reproduced in any form or by any electronic or mechanical means, including information storage and retrieval systems, without written permission from the publisher, except by a reviewer who may quote passages in a review.

British Library Cataloguing in Publication Information Available

Library of Congress Cataloging-in-Publication Data

Manvell, Elizabeth C., 1951–
  Story power! : breathing life into history / Elizabeth Cervini Manvell.
    p. cm.
    Includes bibliographical references.
    ISBN 978-1-60709-919-2

  1. History—Methodology. 2. History—Study and teaching. 3. History—Sources—Study and teaching. 4. Biographical sources—Study and teaching. I. Title.
    D16.2.M3157 2010
    907.1—dc22   2010035707

∞™ The paper used in this publication meets the minimum requirements of American National Standard for Information Sciences—Permanence of Paper for Printed Library Materials, ANSI/NISO Z39.48-1992.

Printed in the United States of America

To families—Van's and my own.

Contents

Acknowledgments		ix
Introduction:	The Power of a Story	xi

Part I **A Natural Connection**

Chapter 1	Learning to Love History	1
Chapter 2	Putting Humanity into History	11
Chapter 3	Sources of Historical Perspective	19
Chapter 4	Types of Sources	27
Chapter 5	Textbooks and Other Non-Primary Sources	35
Chapter 6	Finding the Story	41
Chapter 7	What Do We Need to Teach?	47
Chapter 8	Teachers, the Natural Collectors	53
Chapter 9	Oral Traditions—Tell me about . . .	63
Chapter 10	Making It Formal and Losing the Spirit	67
Chapter 11	Getting Inspired So You Can Inspire	73
Chapter 12	The Find: Historical Thinking at Work	85
Chapter 13	Eking Out the Story	93
Chapter 14	Compelled to Share	99
Chapter 15	Meet the Strong Family	103
Chapter 16	Lydia Writes Home	113

Part II	**History Comes to Life**	
Chapter 17	Van's Story—From Farmer to Fighter	121
Appendix A	The Rest of the Story	163
Appendix B	A Word about Copyright	181

References and Resources — 185
About the Author — 191

Acknowledgments

Story Power! Breathing Life Into History is the culmination of a long journey, a journey only made possible by many people. I wish to express my appreciation to:

- My parents, Mary and Andrew Cervini, for giving me a good start and nurturing my curiosity
- The sixth-grader who brought into school a stack of historic letters that intrigued me
- Three generations of the Showers family: Arlene and Donald, Lisa and David, and Becky, who enthusiastically shared all they knew about their history and Van R. Strong, and treated me like family
- The Library of Congress and other agencies and organizations for being wise enough to continually collect and make available the primary sources of our history
- All the professional historians, teachers, history buffs, antique collectors, and genealogists who are fascinated with history and freely share what they find
- Rowman & Littlefield Education for seeing potential in the original story
- My dear husband, Arthur, who understands how much concentration it takes me to write

Introduction:

The Power of a Story

Let me tell you a story . . .

What memories do these words conjure up for you? Possibly of a story read together on the couch with a parent, your teacher reading to the class, a rainy afternoon cuddled up with a good book, a favorite movie, or an evening around the dinner table swapping tales of what has happened in our lives. These are the wonderful moments of storytelling, when we settle down, with full attention, and really listen.

Stories are everywhere in these intentional moments and in daily life. They engulf us. They inspire us. They chronicle what has happened before to apply to the future. They teach us how to be human. Stories play a major role in our lives—even before we are born. Our life story doesn't start when we arrive. Not at all! We are born into an ongoing story; we are merely a newly introduced character yet to make our contribution.

Our lives are a continuous production of our own personal stories mixed with the tales of others. Love, tragedy, hardship, accomplishments, losses, legacies . . . each of us has a rich story influenced by family heritage, where we live, the people in our life, our standard of living, temperament, education, chance encounters, ironies, lucky breaks and wise choices, nature, and whatever is happening in the world around us at the time. The most average-seeming friends, neighbors, and colleagues could tell us personal stories that would intrigue and even shock us. This is because each life is a constantly changing jumble of experiences, much more complex than what is seen on the surface. When we hear, read, watch, or participate in someone's story, we see the person with new eyes, as a multi-dimensional being, more similar to us than we would have ever guessed, with something meaningful to say.

It is no wonder that personal stories grip us and are so powerful. Anything that applies to our own lives is captivating. As sentient, spiritual, and ego-driven beings, we are always looking for meaning and direction: something with which to judge our own behavior, to see how we stack up. We benefit from both the everyday and extraordinary experiences of other people and learn to empathize with them and grow through their struggles and successes. We can't anticipate how they will affect us; out of their story might come a small idea that touches us in a big way.

The stories can be of strangers or close to home, people who lived long ago or our contemporaries, those who are famous or those who happen to wander into our lives. We do not need to already have a personal connection with the *person* to be interested, because we already have a personal interest in their *story*.

Stories revolve around universal human themes such as self-preservation, relationships, loyalty, survival, and resilience. They are all valuable to us in some way, and when we put them together, we have the complete history of humankind: a history of how people dealt with the never-ending succession of challenges they have always faced.

Stories are also powerful because we can use them to our advantage. All cultures and civilizations have true histories, as well as myths and legends, that are passed down from generation to generation. They are shared in various ways, offering insight and building understanding of who we are and how we came to be. They are a way to preserve culture through a set of values, beliefs, and norms. Storytellers do not get to control the *truth* of what actually happened in the past—truth is reality in its pure form—but as storytellers (historians), they have substantial control over how they tell it and the *message* they choose to send.

Stories—fiction and non-fiction—have certain basic elements in common: setting (time and place), major and minor characters, and a plot with challenges, a climax. and a resolution. Authors put their own spin on how they are told, what is included, what is emphasized, and what is left out. They are in full charge and able to focus on what they feel is important. No wonder it is difficult to distinguish truth from fiction, fact from opinion. Where does one end and the other begin? People can manipulate what is true to suit their needs. It happens all the time. The best we can do is get close to the original source and interpret what we find in as objective a frame of mind as possible.

Stories are powerful teachers because the brain loves narratives: they make us attend. They are easy to follow and remember because they sound familiar. We can relate to their structure and flow. They follow a pattern and make sense in a way that disjointed, individual pieces of information cannot. Teachers, going back to ancient times, have always known this and long used stories to teach a variety of subjects and skills and to pass down their belief systems. So have cultural groups, parents, schools, religions, and governments.

Stories are powerful because our drive to communicate is insatiable, and the magic of storytelling is ageless. Just look around our classrooms, and you see ample evidence of literacy—listening, speaking, reading, and writing—in action.

- Go to any kindergarten classroom, and strike up a conversation with a five-year-old; the stories flow—a creative mixture of reality and a child's ability to make sense of her world.
- Offer first-graders an opportunity to share each morning, and watch as the stories emerge, and you are forced to cut them off.
- Pick up a book and invite third-graders over to the rug to hear a story, and they come running, some of them jockeying to be at your feet.
- Take a tired or overexcited group of middle-schoolers after lunch, and read them a chapter from your read-aloud book. Watch how they settle down and pay attention in a way no amount of cajoling or reprimands could achieve.
- Tell a high school class a personal story from your life, and they are captivated by the intimacy this sharing creates and the insight it gives them into you and into themselves.

It is easy to see how stories are a powerful teaching tool. Starting at a young age, in language development, we listen to others read to us, read the pictures and find a story, read books silently, read aloud, talk about the story, analyze characters, and tell and write our own personal narratives, true accounts, and creative tales. As we advance, we continue to express ourselves creatively, and now also use our literacy skills to figure out and interpret the story as we research and compare information, read critically, support conclusions, and express opinions.

In this book, we look at the power of stories as a means to teach history—ancient, cultural, world, national, familial—and their unique ability to bring students to impressive levels of concentration, deep thought, and conceptual understanding. My examples come from American history as a matter of convenience and for their relevance to my sub-theme of the Civil War, not of nationalism.

On this journey to breathe life into history, you will see examples of primary sources that were available to me and to anyone else interested in research, as you:

- First, hear the story of how a life-long historian was made through early exposure at home and teaching history to her students, and then, beginning in chapter 12, see how an unexpected find elevated history to the level of an avocation.
- View the disciplines that make up the *humanities*, the history of man on earth, and how the specific discipline of *history* is the overarching lens for the study of all the humanities.
- Identify the categories and inherent value of the primary, secondary, and tertiary resources available to us, where to find them, the proper way to use them, and their place in document-based learning.
- Learn the value of primary documents to tell accurate stories and how to establish the validity and reliability of these materials, to distinguish the credible from the flawed, and to use the context and knowledge of the storyteller to critically analyze the message.
- Understand how stories are the natural springboard for in-depth study of historical periods, events, and figures, and that students need to go below the tidy surface to find the real story, where they can analyze and conceptualize.
- Recognize how motivating stories can help us cover the mandated curriculum *and* ensure our students meet and surpass academic performance goals and objectives.
- Learn how letters from a Civil War soldier became the inspiration for an exciting detective story that has spanned more than a decade and continues today.
- Lastly, as an example of breathing life into history, read and enjoy a story, one rich with historical details and insight, gleaned from a real soldier's letters home, corroborated by other authentic documents.

Throughout the book, the underlying goal is to motivate teachers to use authentic materials and stories to become historians themselves and to seek out and be captivated by the tales of people who came before us. Then, as teaching professionals, to use that passion to inspire students to love history so they can apply the insights they gain from the stories to navigate their own private, social, and civic lives.

If we believe the purpose of school is to produce adults who think critically, question what they see and are told, solve problems constructively, believe in our common values, and work for a just society, this approach to learning history as a study of human nature and personal choices is the best way to teach.

Part One:

A Natural Connection

Chapter 1:

Learning to Love History

"We cannot escape history and neither can we escape a desire to understand it."

—Anonymous

He was born in 1919, the first year of peace since World War I broke out in 1916. It was the year prohibition on the sale of alcohol became law and that Congress passed the Nineteenth Amendment, giving women the right to vote. When he was old enough to go to school, the kids on his block used canvas gas mask bags for their schoolbooks, buying them at the Army surplus store for a quarter. The bags were commonplace, and he never gave much thought to their intended use.

Andrew left regular school when he was fourteen, through no choice of his own. He was the oldest of five children, and his mother was seriously ill. He was needed at home in their apartment to take care of her during the day, and so he became the sole teenager in a night school classroom of adults of varying ages and skills instead. His parents were immigrants from northern Italy and wanted all their children to get a good American education. Thus, quitting school altogether was not an option.

The night school principal assigned him to a commercial business course, despite the fact that Andrew's abilities and interests were clearly in other areas. He liked to work with his hands, but typing was not what he'd had in mind.

For six years Andrew walked alone to night school in the early evening, and then back home at eleven P.M. through Harlem in upper Manhattan, where he lived. This was the 1930s, during the tough times of the Great Depression, with its staggering racial and ethnic strife and massive unemployment, especially in Harlem, but this slightly built kid was never bothered by anyone. His favorite distraction as he walked to and from night school was looking in bookstore windows. In Harlem, 125th Street was lined with bookstores. He proudly tells how one of the bookstores was located in the building where President Bill Clinton later set up his offices.

My father is now ninety-one years old, an intelligent man with no formal education beyond the high school diploma he earned in night school. His education didn't stop there, though; he was always an avid reader driven by an intellectual curiosity, and he especially loved history. As a youngster he read adventure and war stories, which he admits became less attractive to him after his World War II duty in the Pacific on a U.S. Navy ship.

It was the history that he loved, the connections he could make to past times and people. One of his sharpest memories as a child was of veterans of the American Civil War marching in a parade in New York City; he also met men who were former slaves. That direct human connection to a war fought in the 1860s, his great-grandparents' generation, on American soil, fascinated him, and it came to have an influence on my life as well.

My family was always up for a Sunday meander to discover something interesting, or for a planned car trip to a specific site. I recently asked my father how he and my mother chose the places we visited on our day trips and vacations when I was a child. He told me they were places they had read or heard about, with a story that interested them, and they shared this curiosity with their three children. With such heartfelt enthusiasm to energize us, our trips to the Civil War battlefields of Gettysburg and Fredericksburg and to the Revolutionary War site Fort Ticonderoga were exciting.

They each had a lasting impact on me, although not in the same way they affected my parents and my older sister and brother, whose greater maturity allowed for more developed understandings of the sites. My experiences were kid-sized, taken in through a child's limited perspective, but I've built on the foundation laid by these experiences throughout my life.

Battlefields weren't the only places we visited. Our destinations included homes of the famous, such as that of James Fennimore Cooper, author of *Last of the Mohicans,* and the rustic Sagamore Hill homestead of Teddy Roosevelt, on Oyster Bay on the north shore of Long Island. I was startled to see President Roosevelt's large animal trophies, which adorned his office—souvenirs from his safaris—and then to later learn of the incongruity that he was a staunch conservationist who created the U.S. Forest Service.

We visited sites that honored the genius and talents of noted Americans, such as Thomas Alva Edison's laboratory in West Orange, New Jersey, and the Baseball Hall of Fame in Cooperstown, New York, where all the greats of

Photo 1.1. Miniature souvenir postcard books. *Author's collection.*

the sport were remembered. We fit in trips to the Pennsylvania Dutch Country to experience the culture, food, and traditions there, and to Mystic Seaport to see the nineteenth-century whaling ships and authentic whaling village, unaware of the pivotal historic event, the Pequot Indian Massacre, that had taken place in the area in 1637.

At other times, it was a natural wonder that drew my parents' attention. We saw dramatic, cascading Niagara Falls and its perpetual rainbow. We visited the St. Lawrence River that serves as the border between New York and Canada, with its canal locks that made it possible for ships to go from the Atlantic Ocean all the way to each of the five Great Lakes. We traveled in the rolling Catskills, home of Washington Irving's lazy Rip Van Winkle; along the historic Hudson River; and to the high peaks in the Adirondack Mountains of northern New York State, where I got my first look at the region's singular-style lawn chairs.

Of special interest was the Skyline Drive in the Blue Ridge Mountains of Virginia, which, for weeks before the trip, I had thought (hoped?) was an aerial amusement park ride. It might as well have been, for all the curves and winding switchbacks we had to maneuver as we skirted and climbed the mountains to the sky. Woefully carsick in the back seat, I was comforted by my mother as I kept my head down, sucked on hard candy, and periodically hung my head near an open window to let the air hit my face. But the excitement of the experience trumped how poorly I was feeling. I was able to enjoy the rural magnificence of Appalachia and the novelty of being in "the South."

Our trips were not extensive or elaborate ones. With a family of five on a limited budget with limited vacation time, our road trips were mostly to sites we could visit in a single day, and during the summer, to those we could see in a handful of days. If you took a compass and drew a circle 600 miles around Freeport, Long Island, you could probably capture most of our destinations.

The federal interstate system was just getting under way back then, so we drove on parkways and two-lane highways, as well as the periodic gravel or dirt road. That was okay with us. We were a map-loving family, and my father, the driver, had a particular penchant for backcountry "shortcuts." They didn't always live up to their name, but we saw a side of the region we would have passed right by, had we stayed on the main roads.

We waved to everyone we passed, especially the young children in their yards, and they waved back. My view of the world was expanded, as I learned that Virginians and Vermonters were people just like New Yorkers, but that not everyone had the same accent, neighbors nearby, or sidewalks to walk on.

There was no such thing as a motel reservation on our trips. We squeezed all we could out of each vacation day and invariably started to look for a motel with a "vacancy" sign after we had already had too much touring. We were tired and hungry, and maybe a little cranky. We stopped at those small mom-and-pop 1950s and '60s motels and little bungalows that sprung up after World War II, with the rise of the family car trip. Each was unique, with plenty of local flavor. The signs proudly advertised their names—*Virginia Gentleman, Jack Frost, Powhatan, Mueller's*—along with amenities such as telephones, heat, free TV, and a restaurant, as well as noting that they were modern and clean! If my begging prevailed and there was a vacancy, we'd choose one with a swimming pool.

I saved up my allowance for weeks before our trips, and my parents always slipped me some extra change to buy souvenirs. Wherever we went, I bought postcards, and small trinkets to remind me of what made the area notable—parchment copies of famous documents, unusual pens and pencils, and miniature postcard books. Bonus souvenirs were interesting rocks, paper placemats decorated with local history and attractions, illustrated packets of table sugar from restaurants, museum brochures, tour maps, and little soaps with the name of the motel on the wrapper. I didn't know at the time that I was collecting *artifacts* to go along with my memories of these historic and scenic wonders.

During this time we were putting together stories of people and regions, events and time periods. Helping us were the ubiquitous roadside historical markers, ready to tell anyone who took the time to stop of an event or a person of some significance. And we did stop, even if it meant circling back to one we had inadvertently driven by. It became a family joke that we couldn't pass up a roadside marker. It was amazing that we made any progress toward our destination, but maybe the signs were our destination.

Most often the signs weren't about an earth-shattering, or even well-known, event or person, but they were always pieces of a local story. These were small tales and bits of information that someone thought warranted notice. Some might not have been "official," state-sanctioned markers, or even completely accurate for that matter, but they gave a sense of the history of the area, providing something to stimulate curiosity. The sign might mention the name of the first European settler; state that a given house was a stop on the Underground Railroad; note that a route was the one John Wilkes Booth took when he fled Washington, D.C.; or mark the site of a great flood, where a wooden bridge floated downstream.

It was on the way to Lake Placid in the Adirondack Mountains to see where the Winter Olympics were once held that I first heard of the abolitionist John Brown, "a-moldering in his grave." We stopped at a historical marker identifying his homestead and burial site, and I heard the story of his failed 1859 raid on the United States Armory and Arsenal at Harper's Ferry, Virginia (later part of West Virginia). Some time after that, we took a trip to Harper's Ferry itself, to experience the place where John Brown took actions against the institution of slavery that many say were the catalyst for the Civil War. I didn't understand all the particulars, but it provided a reference point as I learned American history.

Reading the transcript of his 1859 trial for treason, first degree murder, and inciting an insurrection, compiled from "The life, trial and execution of Captain John Brown known as 'Old Brown of Ossawatomie,'[sic] with full account of the attempted insurrection at Harper's Ferry 1859" (as cited in Linder, Douglas, 2005), I was struck by his statement at sentencing: "Now if it is deemed necessary that I should forfeit my life for the furtherance of the ends of justice, and mingle my blood further with the blood of millions in this slave country, whose rights are disregarded by wicked, cruel, and unjust enactments, I say, let it be done."

Since then, as an adult, I have been back to both places and now understand the significance of the role played by John Brown. His attempt to start a slave rebellion brought the simmering issue to a boil. No one is sure where the original version of the song "John Brown's Body" originated. There have been many subsequent formal and informal versions, with words changed along the way to suit the singer's needs. Put to the tune of "Glory, Glory, Hallelujah," and sung by soldiers as the Union anthem during the war, this first version told the abolitionist's story:

John Brown's body lies a-moldering in the grave,
John Brown's body lies a-moldering in the grave,
But his soul goes marching on.
   Chorus:
Glory, glory, hallelujah,
Glory, glory, hallelujah,
His soul goes marching on . . .

Subsequent early verses honor Brown's sacrifice: "He's gone to be a soldier in the Army of the Lord"; "John Brown's knapsack is strapped upon his back"; "John Brown died that the slaves might be free"; "The stars above in Heaven now are looking kindly down"—and always, "His soul goes marching on" (retrieved from Linder, Douglas, 2005).

There is a reason John Brown was called "Old Brown of Osawatomie," reflecting another side of his life, not celebrated by song. Brown was an abolitionist activist. In 1856, during the struggle to prevent the people of Kansas from determining to become a slave state, amidst the rising tension between pro- and anti-slavery residents, after the attack on the town of Lawrence, the abolitionist center of the state, Brown and his band of like-minded raiders went to Osawatomie, Kansas, and brutally hacked five men to pieces because of their pro-slavery activities.

John Brown's self-expressed purpose on earth was to purge the United States of the blight of slavery, something, he argued, the Bible clearly forbade. He resigned himself to the reality that the only way to destroy this entrenched blight on the nation was through violence. And it turned out that he was right. It took a civil war.

If we dig deep, we find that stories are never as simple or clear-cut as they might appear or as we are taught in school.

What comes back to me from my early family trips is the sense of place, the excitement of the times, and the interesting stories of people who did or tried to do remarkable things, often overcoming great odds. It was during these family adventures that I learned that history was the story of people just living their lives: like Jenny Wade, for example. Visiting Gettysburg,

Pennsylvania, the site of the major Civil War battle and turning point of the war, I was fascinated by the Jenny Wade house and what happened there. It looked like any other eighteenth- or nineteenth-century house in small-town Pennsylvania. But it wasn't. It still had the holes from the stray bullet (*minié* ball) that traveled through two wooden doors, into the kitchen, to kill Jenny while she was baking bread. My own mother loved to bake in our kitchen, so for a child, Jenny's story didn't get any closer to home than that. As the Union and Confederate armies fought on the streets of Gettysburg, Jenny was what we now call collateral damage.

At the Gettysburg National Military Park itself, what struck me most was visiting individual sites where the fighting occurred and learning their unusual names—Devil's Den, the Wheat Field, Peach Orchard, and Little Round Top (which, as the youngest of three, and due to a certain hat I wore, became one of my nicknames). Standing by the field of the infamous, disastrous Pickett's Charge, even at age eight, I sensed this was a terrible day in our history, where something had gone horribly wrong. Children pick up the importance of things from the way their parents and teachers respond to them.

Photo 1.2 Little Round Top battle site, Gettysburg National Military Park. *Author's collection.*

"Genius is 1 percent inspiration and 99 percent perspiration." In West Orange, New Jersey, at the Thomas Edison National Historical Park, this sign, posted next to the time clock in his laboratory, where employees punched in each morning and out each evening, made a lasting impression on me. So did the old phonographs, the early experimental light bulbs and filament materials, the hundreds of test tubes and beakers, the cavernous machine shops, and the simple cot in Edison's library. I knew about cots because I slept on one when we had overnight company. This very cot was where Edison took catnaps so he could get back to inventing whenever the urge struck him, at any time of the day or night.

Edison was a prolific inventor, amassing an impressive 1,093 patents to his name, who, our guide told us, had been kicked out of school for being an incorrigible problem. As a child, used to behaving in school, this gave me a paradox to ponder: Thomas Edison must have been pretty bad to be expelled from school, and yet he had gone on to invent so many important things, things I used every day. I was learning to question what I was told,

Photo 1.3   Thomas Edison memorabilia. *Author's collection.*

to process and evaluate information, and to analyze assumptions. Years later, I learned that Edison was a fast friend of Henry Ford, of automobile fame, who was an outspoken anti-Semite, and this made me wonder about Edison's own views.

At Colonial Williamsburg in Virginia, I was captivated by the story told by the wooden stockades with holes for the head, arms, and legs of sinners and scofflaws who were put to public shame for their misdeeds. Of course, we all tried out the stocks to see what it was like to be held captive like that, unable to get free, open to public ridicule, and exposed to whatever the townsfolk wanted to throw at us. It told me a lot about how society treated its members back in the seventeenth century.

There were also simple lessons of diversity everywhere, such as when my family ate collard greens for lunch in the Williamsburg museum cafeteria, surprised that they were not spinach, as we had thought. Until that day, I had never heard of collard greens. I learned they were a common southern vegetable and began to understand the broader idea that people had different cultures and lived with different natural resources and climates that determined what they grew, ate, and did for a living.

Williamsburg was also a vision of men in powdered wigs and colonial garb and was marked by the pungent smell of the boxwood hedge, formed into an intricate garden maze. I didn't like the smell of the boxwood then, and I still don't; but its smell always connects me to Colonial America.

There was the mention of slaves and the lasting memory of the small country store in Maryland with a sign that said "Whites Only." We didn't have that kind of sign back home, and the hushed tones of my parents told me this was something to note. I was building a concept of what slavery and racial discrimination were about; I was constructing the story for myself.

Most likely, I could not rattle off the *exact* details of these periods in history, except maybe some of those I have studied closely, yet I know where to go to find these particulars if needed. What I do have is context, a framework, the big picture: the time period when things happened, a working understanding of the sequence and causes of events, and the *stories* of some of the public figures and regular people who played a role. I learned of the political, environmental, and social forces at work, how people dressed, what they ate, what they had to work with, and who had the power, and I could then use this information to think and find patterns and to develop understandings that would help me deal with my own life.

By creating a context, history had meaning, and I tucked away the cognitive (thinking) and affective (emotional) parts that touched and intrigued me. These experiences still live in my long-term memory and are a part of *my* history. Over time, a conceptual understanding of history evolved, generated by all the small events and individual people who provided the stories. The human side inspired me to know more, and I grew to find history fascinating, just like my mother and father did. What could be more interesting than stories about real people? I was becoming a student of the humanities, concerned with what humans thought and did, and why they made those choices. My curiosity was piqued. I had learned to love history.

Chapter 2:

Putting Humanity into History

> "Mankind are so much the same, in all times and places, that history informs us of nothing new or strange in this particular. Its chief use is only to discover the constant and universal principles of human nature."
>
> —David Hume

It is no coincidence that the study of people is called the *human*ities, and that this study has long endured as a major focus of academic interest. From history to the arts, music, religion, philosophy, literature, languages, and the law, these disciplines chronicle all that humans have done and created through time.

The humanities stand in sharp contrast to mathematics and the sciences, which concern themselves with things that already exist in nature. We *discover* scientific and mathematical truths and principles through serendipity, or we learn about and come to understand them through study. Gravity, erosion, fusion, fire, time, space, geometry, tessellations, and mechanical advantage have always been in operation. It is our understanding of them and ways to use them for our benefit that have expanded.

In contrast, the humanities are in a continuous process of creation and evolution. They are the living, ever-changing products of human activity and thought. The story of humanity is being written every minute of every day, and we are part of it.

The Ohio Humanities Council (2009) describes humanities as a way of introducing us to the past:

> The humanities are the stories, the ideas, and the words that help us make sense of our lives and our world. The humanities introduce us to people we have never met, places we have never visited, and ideas that may have never crossed our minds.

The humanities explore the ideas people have had, what they did with them, and how they impacted the human condition, past and present. Life is the creative expression of our human consciousness and feelings based on our beliefs, desires, and need to survive and procreate.

History holds a special place in this humanistic legacy. It is the umbrella of all the humanities—the uniting arch. There is a history to everything—music history, art history, the history of law and languages, the history of civilizations and cultures. Investigating the form of government a society chose and its laws, social norms, religions, currents of philosophical thought, scientific beliefs, and artistic creations tells us what those who came before us believed about a supreme being, humanity's purpose on earth, human rights, and the nature of society and power. It also tells us what they thought was important enough to protect, dominate, and fight over.

This is why history *should* have such broad appeal to students—it connects us to the people of past societies and how they viewed and treated *their* world. It mirrors and elucidates what we, and society, face today, the moral dilemmas that permeate a world that is not black and white. History is the choices people once made, and we are aware that our own lives are a succession of large and small, consequential and inconsequential, choices. History is our story.

The humanities, including history, are an integral part of what we have come to call social studies. In 1916 the National Educational Association established a Committee on Social Studies, which called for an interdisciplinary approach to teaching the humanities, such as history, geography, economics, philosophy, and civics, as opposed to focusing on these traditions as separate and unrelated disciplines.

In the 1960s, Jerome Bruner refined and expanded the goal of social studies. He believed teaching is "not a matter of getting [a student] to commit results to mind. Rather, it is to teach him to participate in the process that makes possible the establishment of knowledge . . . knowing is a process, not a product" (Smith, 2002).

Forty-seven years later, Bruner spoke of the power of a story as a teaching tool: "Storytelling performs the dual cultural functions of making the strange familiar and ourselves private and distinctive. If pupils are encouraged to think about the different outcomes that could have resulted from a set of circumstances, they are demonstrating usability of knowledge about a subject" (Crace, 2007).

Bruner's concept of the learning process readily applies to the teaching of social studies and, more specifically, of history. When confronted with a story, we are naturally motivated to construct understanding, not merely to know. Understanding is a product of what we bring to the learning experience and requires us to rectify this with the new concepts we are developing. This process of constructing understanding follows a critical thinking continuum originally identified by the hierarchical steps of Bloom's taxonomy, then revised to express active, less hierarchical processes by Anderson and Krathwohl (2002). This is the cognitive domain of Bloom and Anderson and Krathwohl, where we actively take the following steps:

- *Knowledge/Remember:* Gather information to *create knowledge* to retrieve for further thinking
- *Comprehension/Understand:* Come to know what the information means through interpretation, explanations, expression, and generalizations
- *Application/Apply:* Bring learned facts and concepts to new situations, by comparing and relating them to what we previously believed and making predictions about the future
- *Analysis/Analyze:* Consider them for their essential truths by taking them apart to compare and contrast
- *Synthesis:* Put them back together into logical categories and new creations and designs, bringing ideas together to create new conceptual meaning (Bloom)
- *Evaluation/Evaluate:* Critique and interpret to make informed judgments about what we have learned, judgments we can justify and share with others as we creatively put them to good use in the present and future
- *Create:* Put it all together to use and create new schema, to take what we now know and, on firm ground, explore the uncharted world of "what if" (Anderson and Krathwohl)

The taxonomy compliments the two categories of history education defined by the United States Department of Education: (1) ways of knowing and thinking about history (historical knowledge and perspective) and (2) historical analysis and interpretation. The National Center for History in the Schools (http://nchs.ucla.edu/standards/toc.html) at UCLA supports this belief—that exemplary, comprehensive, high-quality historical study does not emphasize facts over understanding. The Center's standards for history education, in turn, reflect the taxonomy, and define historical thinking as a compliment of five "mutually supportive" skills and abilities:

- Major historical themes
- Chronological periods
- Ways of knowing and thinking about history
- Historical knowledge and perspective
- Historical analysis and interpretation
- Putting historical thinking to work
  (National Center for History in the Schools, 2004)

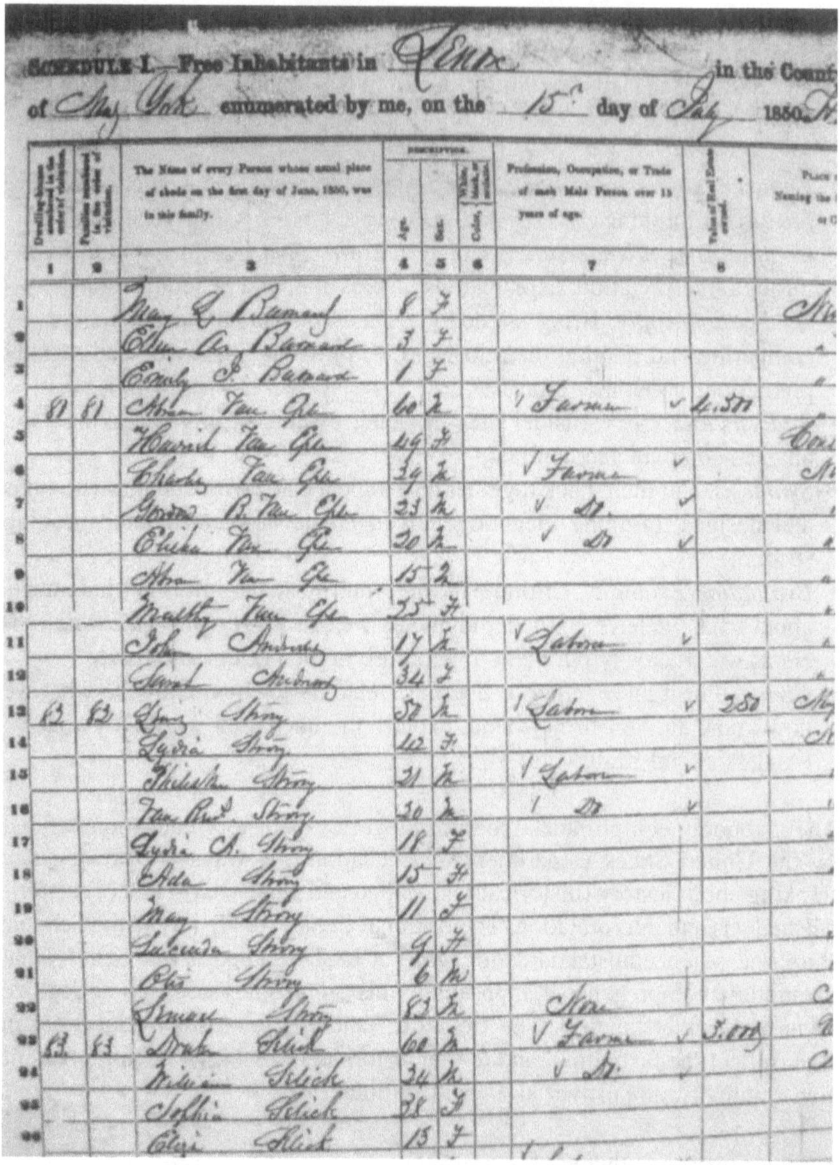

Photo 2.1 Census records are full of historical information. 1850 U.S. Census record for Lenox, Madison County, New York, showing the Van Epps, Strong, and Selleck families in a row. *Courtesy of www.ancestry.com.*

This specific area of the humanities called history is defined as "study that investigates human constructs and concerns" (www.merriamwebster.com). Put another way, the study of history is a critical look at what humans have created, done, said, made, and wrestled with throughout human existence. It is not sufficient to collect historical information as if it were scientific fact or principle. Considering the breadth and depth of what is out there, it is not even a feasible, let alone a preferred, method of inquiry. There is inexhaustible detail to the history of humans on the earth: too much for anybody to study and learn all of it. Instead, we work within a conceptual scheme to help it all make sense, using representative topics such as the following equal rights amendments from "100 Milestone Documents" (www.ourdocuments.gov):

> 15th Amendment to the U.S. Constitution, ratified February 3, 1870
> Section 1. The right of citizens of the United States to vote shall not be denied or abridged by the United States or by any state on account of race, color, or previous condition of servitude.
> Section 2. The Congress shall have power to enforce this article by appropriate legislation.
> 19th Amendment to the U.S. Constitution, ratified on August 18, 1920
> Section 1. The right of citizens of the United States to vote shall not be denied or abridged by the United States or by any state on account of sex.
> Section 2. The Congress shall have power to enforce this article by appropriate legislation.

The Fifteenth Amendment corrected, at least on paper, the injustice done to African American males who were denied stature as citizens and the right to vote. What it also did, though, was blatantly fail to address the glaring lack of such rights for U.S. women of any race.

It took an additional fifty years of continuous pressure, agitation, scorn, and arrests, before Congress passed the Nineteenth Amendment, granting *women* the right to vote. Difficult as it may be to believe, the fact is that the women's suffrage amendment, originally written by Susan B. Anthony and first introduced to Congress in 1878, was not passed by Congress and then ratified by the necessary three-quarters of the states until 1920.

The important issues raised by these two primary documents give us the content and historical perspective through which to learn important thinking skills and universal concepts. They prepare us to think about and analyze any information that presents itself. This is how we evaluate and consolidate information to create broader concepts and essential understandings that apply generally. We are then prepared to tackle whatever comes our way because we can connect it to the concepts and revelations we have internalized.

Now add to this discussion the Equal Rights Amendment to the U.S. Constitution: "Equality of Rights under the law shall not be denied or abridged by the United States or any state on account of sex." Mirroring the women's suffrage amendment, the ERA has been introduced in Congress year after year since 1923, but it still has not been ratified by the necessary margin of state legislatures. The closest it came was in 1972, when it was approved by Congress and sent to the states for ratification. There, it failed to garner the necessary ratification by thirty-eight of the fifty states within the seven-year time limit. The ERA was reintroduced in Congress as recently as July 2009, and there it continues to languish (National Organization of Women, 2009).

Advocates are still hard at work to ensure that the basic human rights of our citizens are protected. Consider this contemporary issue, one of which most of us have not considered or known was happening:

2009 NOW Anti-Shackling Conference Resolution
THEREFORE BE IT RESOLVED, that NOW support state legislation to force detention centers, correctional facilities, and hospitals to discontinue shackling pregnant women who are detained or incarcerated during labor and during pre- and post-childbirth transport from detention to medical facilities; and
BE IT FINALLY RESOLVED, that NOW advocate for legislation to eliminate these dehumanizing and oppressive treatments and policies that impact women who are pregnant, birthing and immediately post-birth. (National Organization for Women, 2010)

Issues and events are never as clear-cut as a summation intimates. Summaries, by their definition, are slim versions of the story. The stories of history are complicated, messy, and not always complimentary to what we hold dear, what we believe about ourselves and our national heritage. They do not easily lend themselves to neat packages.

There is much to consider and dissect in the history of these amendments and resolutions, and that is what history is all about: "learning or knowing by inquiry." This definition of *history* from www.dictionary.com notes that the origin of the word is from the late 1300s Latin and Greek word *historia*, and historia is a derivation of the word *histore*: one who knows or sees. The message is clear: as with the issue of women's rights, historians go past the information to the analysis of the information. They engage in an active process of searching and knowing. This process requires that we move beyond the lower level of Bloom's taxonomy, where history education too often gets bogged down.

Granted, we need a base of knowledge and comprehension of historical themes and chronological periods, as advised by the U.S. Department of Education, but we also must acknowledge the paramount need to apply reasoning to these basics we know—names, places, dates, and events—and approach with skepticism and scrutiny what might appear to be *absolutes* and *givens*. Taking information and wrestling with it means having assumptions and misinformation shattered, to exist in a world of "maybe" and "perhaps" and "I really don't know," and to enjoy and even choose to live there.

This wonderfully enlightening realm of swirling ideas and questions is the gray area teachers tend to avoid when pressed to cover grand social studies curricula in unreasonable timeframes, worrying how well their students will perform on tests and even how much they will be paid as a result of their students' scores.

Chapter 3:

Sources of Historical Perspective

"If history is a collection of events which come to life for us because of what some actors did, some recorders recorded, and some previewers decided to retell, a clinician attempting to interpret an historical event must first of all get the facts straight."

—Erik Erikson

There are many decisions to make before we can go on a journey teaching history. Where do we get the historical information to comprehend, interpret, analyze, apply, synthesize, and evaluate? How do we find it? And is all historical information of equal value or importance? Is it accurate? Biased? Corroborated? Thorough? And then to what in particular do we narrow our study, and how will we learn the content well enough to apply a healthy degree of insight and skepticism as we teach it to others?

True historians are open-minded, more dedicated to the truth than tied to an ideology. We have discussed the idea that people are subjective souls with their own personal stories, which subsequently affect their interpretation of the stories of others. Nothing we are told is ever the pure "truth." Truth is a concept of the ideal, the actuality of a matter that is indisputable and can be empirically verified. As soon as we introduce people and the passage of time into the equation, intentionally and unintentionally, bias creeps in. Much of what is portrayed as the truth is, in reality, a subjective view of what might have originally started out as verifiable facts. Facts, data, research findings, and statistics can be manipulated to fit a particular need. And even that manipulation and the motives behind it provide us with fascinating information to digest.

Consider the source. It is an adage we are familiar with. We consider the source regularly in our personal lives, where we are exposed to and know the sources well—family, friends, co-workers, local political leaders, even talk show hosts—and can easily consider their personalities, biases, and motives. Thinking people aim to apply skepticism to all aspects of their lives. We are less apt or able to apply the adage when the source is unknown or the topic is complex and foreign to us. As Pieter Geyl assesses it, "Imagination plays too important a role in the writing of history, and what is imagination but the projection of the author's personality" (Szasz, Ferenc M., n.d.).

A skeptical view is healthy and should not be confused with a negative or closed-minded attitude. Skepticism helps us avoid being manipulated or misled by the stories we are told. It helps us recognize yellow journalism and propaganda that vie for our attention through sensational and simplistic views of current events and aim to do the thinking for us. The cautious approach of the skeptic is especially important as we study history, where we need to ask:

- Who is the bearer of the information? What is our relationship with this source?
- Is she in a position to have this information? Is she an expert?
- How many steps removed is she from the original source?
- How reliable has she been in the past?
- Does the bearer have a strong bias for or against the topic? Is it a personal issue for her?
- What is her motive?
- How does she benefit from sharing the information?
- Is someone paying her to say it? Who is bankrolling the effort?
- Is the information presented as a fact, the truth, or an opinion?
- Can the information be verified? How does it compare with other primary sources?
- Given what we know, do we agree, or are we skeptical?

To learn about the past, it is essential that we seek reliable information from reputable sources. With the proliferation of information on the Internet and the free access to both quality and questionable sources, the scrutiny and documentation of sources become even more important. There is no end to the electronic information stream. We are blessed with a treasure trove at our fingertips, where we don't need to leave our homes, offices, or classrooms. But websites hosted by organizations are rife with bias. They have a story to promote, points to make, and even contributions to collect.

Do some background checking. Many websites provide an *About the Author* section that can be revealing and useful in determining where the person is coming from and whether he or she is an expert in the field. Never pass up the chance to learn about who is teaching you. Read the *About Us* and *Home* pages and you'll be able to better assess their philosophical bent and goals.

Each of us has likely used Wikipedia.com for an introduction to a topic or a quick answer to a burning question. In our minds, we know this is an open forum, where anyone with a desire can post information . . . but it *is* a convenient entry-level resource. Wikipedia information might legitimately serve as a useful base *if* we pay attention to the secondary sources, or lack thereof, each contributor has cited.

The Wikipedia organization itself is concerned with the validity of the materials on its site. Their "Identifying Reliable Sources" page states, "The threshold for inclusion in Wikipedia is verifiability, not truth. 'Verifiable' in this context means that any reader should be able to check that material added to Wikipedia has already been published by a reliable source."

Their criteria for such a reliable resource is that it be a legitimate *published* resource from a reputable organization known for fact-checking that is accepted by scholars. They identify their articles as "tertiary sources" (the same as an encyclopedia or textbook) and caution that they "should not be used as sources within articles" (Wikipedia: Identifying reliable sources, 2010).

If a researcher wants to use the information contained in Wikipedia, he should only use those entries that are referenced, and then only as a lead to the secondary source where the information can be verified. If possible, trace back to the primary sources the secondary source used.

The genealogy website ancestry.com is another popular open-source site where we can find generally sound and hard-to-find information. As with Wikipedia, individuals are able to post information they have compiled, in this case about their family, from primary and secondary documents and artifacts. As we use these sites, it is advisable to take into account the powerful human drive to connect the dots. As much as contributors have the opportunity and are encouraged to cite and post primary sources, they also have the flexibility to post information derived from supposition, family lore, insufficient research, inaccurate interpretations, and faulty reasoning. I was very aware of this as I conducted my research for the Civil War soldier part of this book.

To our benefit, many open-source sites have set standards and a way for the user to assess the validity of the information. Claims on a site like ancestry.com include source citations. The absence of a citation is a red flag to not trust the material as reliable. Typically, contributors have done their research and substantiate their claims with links to actual primary documents, usually accessible on the entry's webpage itself. Good information is referenced with a photocopy of the document from such sources as official U.S. census records; U.S. military and other government records; public birth, death, marriage, and real estate records; ship manifests and immigration records; gravesites; and news reports from the times.

Used carefully, genealogy sites are a great way to piggyback off the efforts of others as we seek to learn about a topic and identify motivating materials to use with our students. Such genealogical information gleaned from ancestry.com was invaluable to me as I put together a historically verifiable story of my Civil War soldier. Familysearch.org is another comprehensive genealogy service provided by the Church of Jesus Christ of the Latter Day Saints. It applies no religious filter to the massive collection of primary records it offers free to the public.

Faced with the realities of wikis—open-source websites—we are forced to ask ourselves whether it is wise to aim so low and take unnecessary chances when the Internet gives us almost endless access to primary and secondary materials through reputable, scholarly, not-for-profit, and local and state government websites. Comprehensive, reliable collections of firsthand primary documents exist on the Internet in an amazing spectrum of topics. Museums, national historical sites, universities, libraries, and historical societies have much to offer, whether you visit them in person or on their websites. Universities often receive generous donations of extensive private collections of primary materials that they then make available digitally to researchers. The topics are as varied and esoteric as history itself.

One such remarkable digital collection is the *Thomas A. Edison Papers Project* at Rutgers University in New Jersey. It exemplifies the extent of primary information available to us if we just look for it. Since 1978, Rutgers has been working to make available to the public the five *million* pages of Edison-related primary documents they hold—some of them the property of the Edison National Historical Park. This collection allowed me to go beyond the myth of Edison's public persona to a glimpse of who he was as a human being.

My childhood fascination with Edison was recently revived when I visited this site and discovered a diary he wrote during the summer of 1885. I always thought of Edison as the brilliant "Wizard of Menlo Park," preoccupied with scientific thought, always working and inventing. (Remember the cot?) I had bought the representation of the man as an icon and was therefore surprised to find his writing down to earth, insightful, and quite witty:

- Woodside Villa, July 16, 1885: "If this weather gets much hotter hell will get up a reputation as a summer resort."
- Sunday July 12, 1885: "Holzer is going to the old laboratory for the purpose of hatching chickens artificially by an electric incubator . . . —Just think electricity employed to cheat a poor hen out of the pleasures of maternity—Machine born chickens. What is home without a mother" (Edison, Thomas, 1885).

- July 20, 1885, during the blazing heat of the summer and feeling most uncomfortable, Edison wrote, "it's so hot I put everything off—hot weather is the mother of procrastination"—a clever twist on the saying, "Necessity is the mother of invention," a well-known proverb that actually originated with the ancient Greek philosopher Plato.

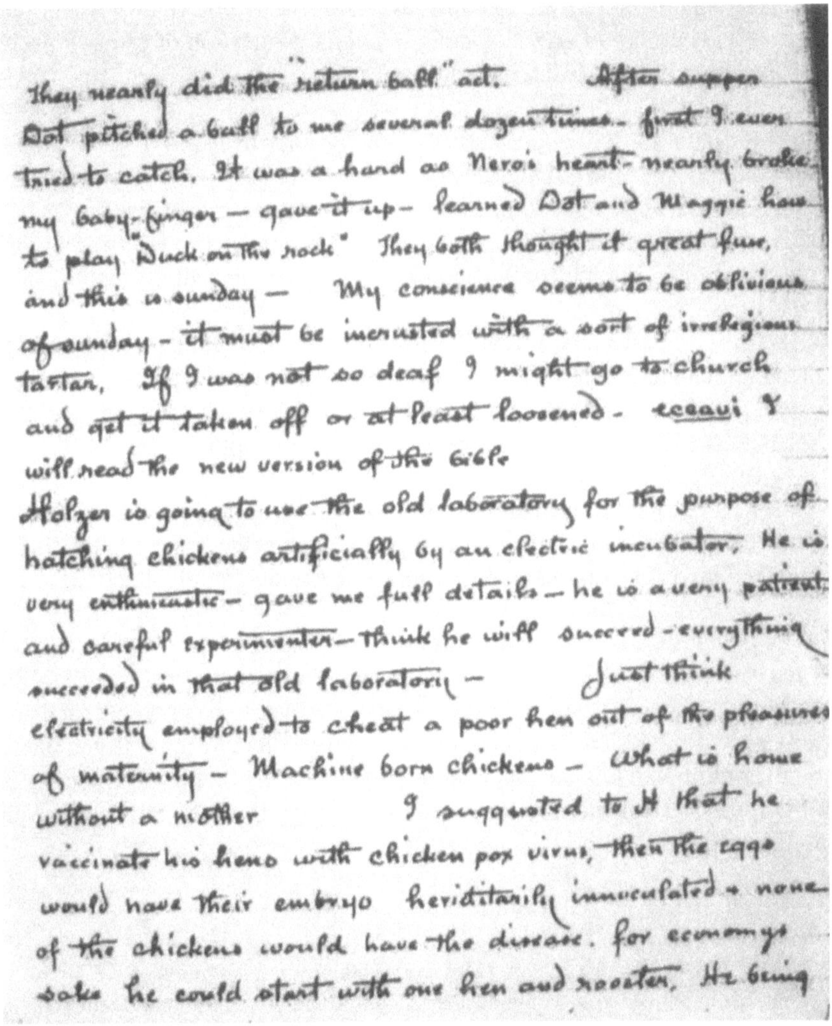

Photo 3.1 Thomas Edison's July 12, 1885, "incubator" diary entry. *Courtesy of the U.S. Department of Interior, National Park Service, Thomas A. Edison National Historical Park.*

The National Digital Newspaper Program, Chronicling America, found at www.neh.gov/projects/ndnp, is a collaboration between the National Endowment for the Humanities and the Library of Congress. This website offers us open access to historic newspapers, saving a trip to a library to scroll through microfiche. The result is a searchable database of U.S. newspapers—an amazing collection of primary source material.

Search a specific subject or browse a university's online library, and you will likely find what you are looking for or something you can use. This was the case as I explored Duke University's Digital Collection of primary materials available online, which includes:

- Women of the Civil War special collection: *The Alice Williamson Diary*, revealing the thoughts and experiences of a sixteen-year-old girl living in Union-occupied Gallatan, Tennessee, during the last full year of the Civil War.
- Trent Collection of Whitmaniana: Walt Whitman's own handwritten drafts of his mid-nineteenth-century poems, with his self-corrections and revisions.
- Historical American Sheet Music from 1850–1920, with sheet music for Civil War songs, including "You are Going to the Wars," "Secession Quickstep," "The Drummer Boy of Shiloh," "The Slave's Consolation" (or "I'll Neber Hoe de Cotton Any More"), "The Patriot Mother's Prayer: Protect My Boy."
- Advertising and Consumer Culture: the Medicine and Madison Avenue collection of advertising and other primary documents, from 1911 to 1958. (Duke University Libraries, http://library.duke.edu/digitalcollections)

The University of Washington Libraries' digital database includes a Civil War Letters Collection that is mesmerizing. You can get lost studying the miniature photographs taken during the first war ever to be photographed and reading diaries and letters written to and from soldiers, from both the North and the South, like this one from Samuel D. Lougheed to his wife, Jennie, in April 1862. Here, he describes the aftermath of the Battle of Pittsburg Landing (Shiloh):

April 20, 1862
Pittsburg Landing, TN
... I would like to give you many very many more particulars of the late & great battle; but I fear it would awaken feelings, and emotions, apart from pleasure in your mind. I will only mention two or three incidents which will enable you to form some idea of the terrible destruction of human life on both sides. In some graves we burried [sic] as many as 40 of our own soldiers, side by side, and

one on top of the other. In others we buried of the rebel soldiers killed in battle as high as 140 in one grave and some pits may have had more in than that.
(Lougheed, 1862)

In another letter to his wife, dated October 7 of that year, Samuel is broken by the horrors he has witnessed and pines for a quick end to the conflict. It was not to be. Samuel and Jennie had to endure three more years of war.

Another fine example of such a university collection, invaluable to my Civil War research, is Cornell University's *The Making of America*. The digital library site contains primary documents for many time periods, including the antebellum South through Reconstruction after the war. During the war itself, army officers were required to keep detailed records of each day's events and to send them to their superior officer with due speed.

The resulting collection, *The War of the Rebellion: A Compilation of the Official Records of the Union and Confederate Armies from the United States*, makes available all the U.S. War Department Civil War field reports and communications by the military leaders from both the North and the South, for the entire four-year duration of the war. What an assemblage of firsthand accounts and potential insight this is! You can read exactly what was written on the battlefield, on the march, or in camp, by those who were there.

It was a well-documented war. Everyone seemed to be writing, and letters were sent back and forth uncensored. The Union and Confederate enlisted men and officers out in the field and their loved ones at home were avid letter-writers and readers, trying to stay in touch the only way they had available, other than by telegram. The soldiers shared their daily life, troop movements, battle experiences, lack of food, and longing for home and family. Loved ones at home told them of their own worries, news of visits with friends, condition of crops, and finances, and of their children left behind.

Officers, following army protocol, had no choice other than to also communicate regularly with their superiors and to keep accurate records of battles, supplies of munitions and food rations, and of the dead, injured, ill, and missing soldiers of their units. These reports benefited the federal government as well as the armies out in the field, and now provide us with invaluable firsthand accounts and raw data.

Although personal letters and official reports are firsthand accounts written in the line of duty, they, too, are to be consumed with analytical scrutiny. Soldiers were writing letters to a specific audience—parents, siblings, wives, friends, and children. What they said was a product of their individual characters and perspectives. It stands to reason that the side of the conflict for which they were fighting prejudiced the writing of both soldiers and officials, but even this should not be assumed.

To spare their loved ones, enlisted men might choose to minimize or not to mention the danger and suffering they endured—or they might choose to share it openly and express their deep feelings about the war and their loneliness. The military men who authored official reports had reason to embellish their or their fighting units' successes and bravery and to minimize lapses in judgment or unsuccessful strategies. It was in the best interest of their careers and reputations, and for public support for the war, to do so.

To complicate this challenge of sorting fact from opinion, the style of writing during that time period was more effusive, sentimental, and prone to exaggeration, than is currently typical. Even official military reports reflect this. Here is a letter from Colonel Marsh of the 20th IL Infantry, thanking the 46th IL Volunteer Infantry, my soldier's regiment, for their bravery at the Battle of Shiloh in Tennessee. According to Timothy T. Isbell in his book *Shiloh and Corinth: Sentinels of Stone* (as cited in civilwar.ilgenweb.net/history/046.html) and various regimental histories, the 46th Illinois was known as the Davis Regiment, and their well-liked Colonel John A. Davis was, after having two horses shot out from under him, seriously injured in the Battle of Shiloh (Pittsburg Landing) and carried off the field.

> Headquarters Second Brigade, First Division
> April 9th, 1862
>   Dear Sir:—I beg to thank you and the officers and soldiers of the Forty-sixth Illinois Infantry for their noble conduct during the action of Monday morning last, when your lamented Colonel so promptly responded to my request to take a position in my command, and so gallantly led you in the face of the enemy with so fatal a result to himself. My heartfelt sympathies are with you in your severe loss, and your soldierly conduct shall receive a fitting notice in my official report.
> I am, sir, truly yours.
> C.C. Marsh
> Colonel Twentieth Illinois Infantry, Commanding Brigade
> (Adjutant General's Report, n.d.)

These eyewitness descriptions of military engagements and the communications between officers and the War Department are riveting and revealing. They remain the unabridged, raw history of the times, *as interpreted by the people who were there*. That is the part we must remember.

Chapter 4:

Types of Sources

"Skepticism is history's bedfellow."

—Edgar Saltus

It becomes clear, then, why, when studying history, validity and reliability are critical tests. The written word is a minefield of bias planted intentionally or subconsciously by whoever tells the story. All sources are not of the same caliber.

One way to avoid the bias inherent in a retelling and the passage of time, or at least to be able to recognize the bias, is to verify the claims by examining original materials. This is a worthwhile investment of our time, both as a mental exercise that builds intellect and as a life skill, practical to us as we lead our lives. This process stimulates historical thinking and makes us savvy evaluators of information.

Once we locate a source, the next step is to research the source itself, identify whether it is a primary or secondary source, and compare the information put forth to claims made by others. An individual source does not speak for all people. Comparing and contrasting personal perspectives and accounts helps us maneuver through the overwhelming abundance of information out there at our disposal.

Simply stated, a primary source is one created at a specific time in history by someone who was there to experience it herself. It is a firsthand account, impression, or artifact. Secondary sources are written by others who were not there to experience it themselves. The creators of secondary sources study and interpret primary sources and draw conclusions about the story the primary documents tell.

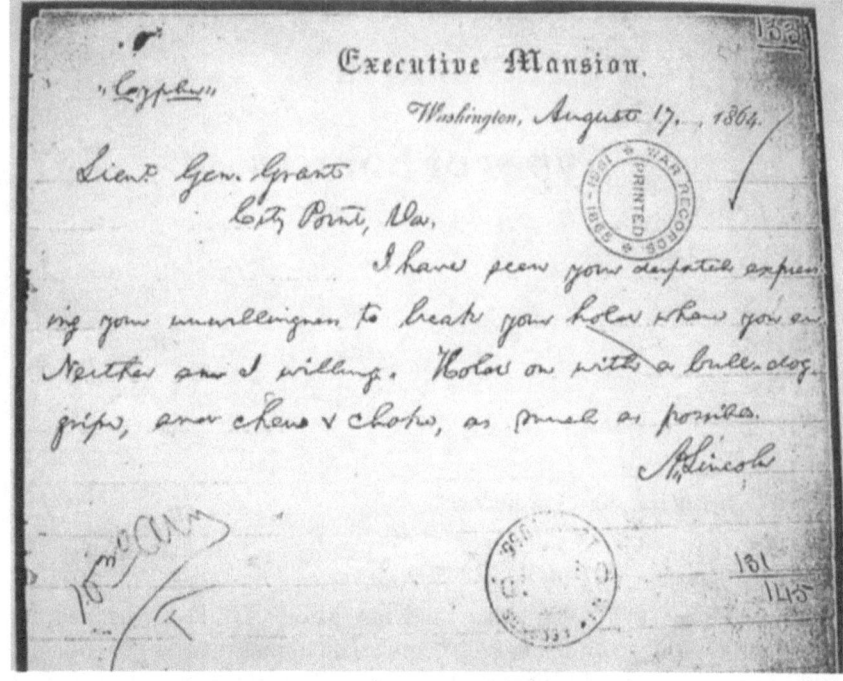

Photo 4.1 August 17, 1864, telegram from President Lincoln telling Lt. General Ulysses S. Grant at Petersburg to "Hold on with a bulldog grip, and chew and chop, as much as possible." *Courtesy National Archive and Records Administration "American Originals" Exhibit.*

This book is based both on primary materials and secondary sources and includes some of my personal stories. In that context, when I share my family history and artifacts and explain my contemporary quest to interpret the original Civil War letters I acquired, it is in part a memoir and autobiographical. Within the pages of *Story Power,* I include images of a sampling of the original primary documents I used to write the book and note the secondary sources I read and used as background resources.

The Regents of the University of California do a good job of defining primary and secondary sources. In their article "Distinguish between Primary and Secondary Sources," they state, "The type of information and the source of the information establish its authenticity and value," and include three critical questions to ask:

1. How does the author know these details (names, dates, times)? Was the author present at the event or soon on the scene?

2. Where does this information come from—personal experience, eyewitness accounts, or reports written by others?
3. Are the author's conclusions based on a single piece of evidence, or have many sources—diary entries, third-party eyewitness accounts, impressions of contemporaries, and newspaper accounts—been taken into consideration? (Distinguish Between Primary and Secondary Resources, n.d.)

A primary document is a single piece of evidence of the personal or official experience of someone present during the event, while secondary sources are reports of the events written by others not present who used multiple primary resources to draw conclusions. Many types of materials meet the criteria for primary resources. These firsthand accounts consist of:

- Official and legal records (censuses, birth, death, and marriage records, court transcripts and decisions, citizenship papers, Congressional and other government records).
- Published materials from the time (newspapers, articles, essays, speeches, advertisements, maps, campaign materials, Internet postings, blogs, and other social media).
- Unpublished documents (letters, diaries, business records, memos, e-mail, telegrams, poems, essays).
- Audio and visual documents (artistic creations, photographs, movies, raw footage, oral histories, illustrations, cartoons, murals, radio broadcasts, recorded interviews, posters, advertisements).
- An endless array of physical objects called artifacts (personal items, jewelry, cooking utensils, tools, clothing, carvings, weapons, souvenirs, toys, pottery, machines, medical implements, architecture, individual collections).
- Memoirs, autobiographies, interviews, and other materials created after-the-fact by those who were there to experience it firsthand.

The task is more challenging when you study ancient civilizations and world cultures with languages other than your own. Even so, the basic principles apply to all historical study. This is why reliable secondary resources, compiled by those who can read and translate the primary documents for us, are invaluable.

Researchers benefit from global Internet sites such as the World Digital Library (WDL) and the Internet History Sourcebooks Project from Fordham University. The World Digital Library is a "cooperative project of the Library of Congress, the United Nations Educational Scientific and Cultural Organization (UNESCO), and partner libraries, archives, and educational and cultural institutions from the United States and around the world. The project brings together on a single website rare and unique documents—books, journals, manuscripts, maps, prints and photographs, films, and sound recordings—that tell the story of the world's cultures" (www.loc.gov/wdl).

The WDL lets you browse in seven languages, and documents are presented in their original languages. You can search by time, place, topic, type of item, and institution, as well as click on the interactive world map to access relevant primary documents from any continent and country. The archives include everything from an 1896 map of the Belgian Congo to "On the Calculation of Numbers in the Science of Astronomy from Eighteenth-Century Timbuktu," and the 1698 "An Account of a Voyage up the River de la Plata, and Thence Over Land to Peru: With Observations on the Inhabitants, as well as Indians and Spaniards; the Cities, Commerce, Fertility, and Riches of that Part of America" (www.wdl.org).

The Internet History Sourcebooks Project global resource site at Fordham University, edited by Paul Halsall (www.fordham.edu/halsall), includes public domain and copy-permitted historical texts for educational use organized by ancient, medieval, and modern history, countries, and areas of interest. A sampling of the array of documents include "The Constitution of Carthage by Aristotle" (c. 340 BCE), "Ancient Accounts of Arabia" (430 BCE–550 CE), Columbus' 1494 letter to the king and queen of Spain, and Commodore Matthew Perry's 1854 account "When We Landed in Japan."

As primary source information ranks highest in inherent historical value, who better than the Library of Congress to express with clarity and passion the importance of primary documents? It is the people's library, a national repository holding 145 million items on 745 miles of shelves, and it adds approximately 10,000 items to the collection each day (Library of Congress Fascinating Facts, www.loc.gov/about/facts.html).

The Library of Congress explains it this way:

> Primary sources provide a window into the past—unfiltered access to the record of artistic, social, scientific and political thought and achievement during the specific period under study, produced by people who lived during that period. Bringing young people into close contact with these unique, often profoundly personal, documents and objects can give them a very real sense of what it was like to be alive during a long-past era. (Why Use Primary Resources? n.d.)

The Library of Congress (LOC) *American Memory* digital collection is exhaustive in scope. Go there to find amazing resources on immigration, women's history, maps, African-American history, religion and advertising, and much more (http://memory.loc.gov/ammem). They also have a main reading room for researchers in the Humanities and Social Services Division (www.loc.gov/rr/main) and a separate section devoted to teachers (www.loc.gov/teachers). This teaching strand fosters the use of primary documents as a means of teaching history in an authentic way. They provide primary source sets of documents, photographs, audio files, and teacher guides on such topics as *Dust Bowl Migration, Assimilation Through Education, Hispanic Exploration, Jim Crow in America,* and *Westward Expansion.*

The LOC offers powerful justifications for using primary resources. They engage students in the process of historical thought while guiding them to develop analytic skills and offering them the time and encouragement to construct knowledge and understanding. They tout primary resources as "snippets" of history, incomplete with no built-in context. To use such documents, students have their work cut out for them, and this is a good thing.

They have even expanded access to their holdings to Photostream on Flickr, where you can locate photographs from their collections and communicate with LOC staff to share information you have regarding the photograph. In one case, a photograph labeled Susan B. Anthony was of another suffragette, and the error was corrected (www.flickr.com/photos/Library_of_Congress).

Digital audio, digital visual, and print primary source materials are available for sale at the National Archives Store (estore.archives.gov) for a nominal fee of a few dollars. A sampling of the original audio files you can download relating to people, places, and events in American history include:

- An April 11, 1962, recording of John Glenn discussing his historic orbit in space.
- Thomas A. Edison talking about the future of electricity in 1908.
- A 1944 radio dramatization about World War II rationing coupons and prices of goods.
- William Faulkner's December 10, 1950, musings about the future of man.
- A commercial for the 1943 "War Against Waste Day."
- The actual first telephone conversation heard around the world on April 14, 1935.
- Remarks made by runner Jesse Owens at the 1936 Olympics held in Nazi Germany.
- Ernest Hemingway talking about the loneliness of the writer.
- A reporter's eyewitness account of the executions at Nuremberg, Germany.

Just think how relevant these sources are to contemporary life and how motivating they could be for students.

Sometimes, just browsing these sites leads to exciting discoveries. Included in the holdings of Cornell's *Making of America* are original pieces written on issues important to understanding our history. I happened on a pre-Civil War essay, "Slavery and the Slave Trade," by Horace Dresser, in which he questions the right of the federal government to eliminate a state's right if that right is *not* expressly prohibited by the U.S. Constitution. It provides eye-opening insight into the Southern argument for the supremacy of states' rights over federal law and of white men over African-American men and women.

With none of the enlightenment of the twenty-first century to hold the writer back, this article, published in *The United States Democratic Review* in 1859—the same year John Brown raided Harper's Ferry—presents a starkly rational discussion of the legality of the institution of slavery. It is clinical, devoid of concern with the paradox or rightness of an arrangement where one human owns another human as property, to buy and sell and do with as one would a horse or a cord of wood. It actually advances the belief that as Africans were not truly human, owning them would not be an act against God or humanity.

The author concludes, since the federal government cannot take away a person's property, "That there is no power in the United States government, nor in that of any of the States, to divest a citizen of his ownership of or control over his slave" (p. 347). He further argues the claim that African Americans have no legal status in America, writing "That upon inauguration of this government under the Constitution, none but white persons became citizens of the United States" (p. 348).

To the privileged of the South, whose agrarian economy was dependent on large, profitable farms (plantations) that required hundreds of workers, the bottom line was that a slave was property and a tool of business, not a citizen with rights, and only a tyrannical government would try to interfere. While abolitionists in the industrial, commerce-centered North championed freedom for slaves based on a sense of social justice, religious teachings, and a shared humanity, the agrarian Southern secessionists presented arguments based on tradition, business, free enterprise, and interpretation of constitutional law (Dresser, Horace, 1859).

This primary resource allows us to hear an uncensored argument from one of Lincoln's contemporaries and to gain insight into how the Southern states justified seceding from the Union. When the Constitution or federal law was silent on an issue, Southerners put states' rights above those of the federal government. They were not arguing the merits of slavery, as were the abolitionists. Rather, they argued the right to own slaves without government interference. Through this authentic essay from a thinker of the times, we have new primary information to consider. Then, as true historians, we can use critical thinking to construct our own understanding and opinions of the arguments.

In the spirit of "considering the source," my research revealed that the *United States Democratic Review* was a pro-slavery publication.

Photo 4.2 Antietam, Maryland. Allan Pinkerton, President Lincoln, and Maj. Gen. John A. McClernand; October 3, 1862. *Courtesy of the Library of Congress, Prints and Photographs Division, Civil War Photographs [reproduction number LC-DIG-cwpb-03803].*

Chapter 5:

Textbooks and Other Non-Primary Sources

"Who does not know that the first law of historical writing is the truth?"

—Cicero

Investigating the types of resources historians and students use led me to a compelling book by James W. Loewen, *Lies My Teacher Told Me: Everything Your American History Textbook Got Wrong* (Loewen, 1997). Loewen believes that the further we remove ourselves from the original source, the more risk there is for pre-digestion and bias by others. This is especially true of textbooks—tertiary sources—that take chunks of time and human events and digest them, pare down, and condense them, draw conclusions, and then present the material as fact. We are taught what is most palatable and time efficient. Loewen's thoroughly researched unraveling of the simplistic and inaccurate stories we are taught about our history should be required reading for all Americans and certainly all teachers (homepage of James W. Loewen: sundown.afro.illinois.edu/).

In their naiveté, teachers and students assume that extensive research and critical review has gone into the creation of a textbook, that it is carefully researched and supported by primary sources, and that nothing false or slanted could have squeaked through such scrutiny and made it into print. We know we aren't experts, so we trust that the textbook authors and editors are and that they are unbiased and work with ample safeguards in place.

Is this trust warranted? Not really. The fox is alive and well in the henhouse. We cannot rely on the viewpoints expressed by textbook authors and editors, who are individuals with personal biases and motives; they write something that appeals to the widest audience, and their bottom line is to make money.

A textbook is a long way from the personally relevant process of studying the authentic writings, objects, and artifacts of times past and making sense of them for yourself. Textbooks do not meet the criteria of a "scholarly work."

Loewen labels it the "universal processed voice of the history textbook," which he claims "insulates us from the raw materials of history." He challenges us to skip the middlemen and get right down to the original "speeches, songs, diaries, and letters that make the past come alive" (from the introduction to *Lies My Teachers Told Me* on the homepage of James W. Loewen, n.d., para. 18).

Sanitized history from a limited perspective, no matter how organized, detailed, well-written, attractively illustrated, or seemingly balanced, is not a recommended source from which to teach our students. We would never knowingly teach misinformation, but it is a matter of being misinformed. Using tertiary resources—shorthand compilations of information, like textbooks, encyclopedias and wikis—as the basis of instructional material is more of a decision of expedience and a lack of our own knowledge and understanding of the content. Textbooks are organized and convenient. It is easy to hang onto them like a crutch because they are time-savers. The work is already done for us.

For decades, it was widely known that the state of Texas was the driving force behind the changing content and perspectives in our nation's textbooks. With such a huge market, the publishers worked hard to please them by preparing textbooks Texas would condone and buy, containing and omitting content so the resulting entries agreed with their ideology. These national texts were then sold in other states, and thus Texas's influence spread. Things have changed somewhat. With the rise of state standards, which led to state-standardized tests, a one-size-fits-all history textbook no longer meets all educators' needs.

In his March 26, 2010, *Texas Tribune* article, "The Textbook Myth," author Brian Thevenot asserts that even though Texas and a few other large states no longer have a stranglehold on the textbook industry, the process through which texts are published still strikes the lowest common denominator by avoiding anything controversial that might negatively affect sales (Thevenot, 2010, para. 24).

The article quotes Eric Foner, historian, professor, and author of the *Give Me Liberty* history text, as saying, "No self-respecting historian would change their version of U.S. history just because the Texas school board says so" (Thevenot, 2010, para. 23). While intending to debunk the myth of large state influence on what is taught, Foner actually identifies the problem. Many K–12 history textbooks are not written by self-respecting historians; they are written by large committees, who Thevenot calls "hired hands," and are subjected to the whims of the powerful-in-charge. Thevenot calls the resulting books "the chicken nuggets of the literary world"—highly processed and barely reminiscent of the original—and he brings up a critical concern about what is left out of textbooks (Thevenot, 2010, para. 24). Thevenot writes, "And perhaps even more than what state board members add to the curriculum, what they have deleted, including references to church-state separation and minority and feminist figures, may end up having more effect on what students do—and do not—learn from their history books" (Thevenot, 2010, para. 9).

In an NPR broadcast of City Arts and Lectures recorded on April 12, 2010, Mark Danner, author of many books including his newest, *Stripping Bare the Body: Politics, Violence, War,* made an observation that is now burned into my mind, and I paraphrase: With the simple stories we are fed, we don't worry too much about facts; the belief comes first, gathering the facts to support the belief comes afterward (Mark Danner and Frank Rich in conversation, April 12, 2010).

And to this I add, how many people ever make that effort to gather the facts? The simplistic version sums it up just fine, thank you. We let other people do the thinking for us and say, "Ditto."

Previously, we said a true historian has the integrity to keep an open mind as she compares and contrasts primary documents and presents serious analysis of what she finds, absent an ideology that narrows her thinking. In the ideal, the true historian is a truth seeker who reads sources from all perspectives not just to support her premise. Historians have to be above reproach, and this is especially true when choosing what the next generation of American children will and will not be taught. Most textbooks do not hold up to this standard.

A wiser way to teach is to use the trustworthy individuals and organizations dedicated to providing materials and that allow you and your students to draw conclusions. Viable historical primary resources come from a variety of universally recognized authorities that have a commitment to objectivity and integrity. The National Park Service and other U.S. governmental agencies offer us a promise by way of a set of standards for the quality of the material they disseminate. In Directors' Order #11B: *Ensuring Quality of Information Disseminated by the National Park Service,* effective October 2002, Congress directed the Office of Management and Budget (OMB) to:

> provide policy and procedural guidance to Federal agencies for ensuring and maximizing the quality, objectivity, utility, and integrity of information (including statistical information) disseminated by Federal agencies.
> (www.nps.gov/policy/DOrders/11B-final.htm)

The OMB even goes a step further in its attempt to get history right. They define administrative mechanisms to allow individuals to seek and obtain correction of information maintained and disseminated by the agency when that information does not comply with guidelines issued by the OMB. If anything is proven to be incorrect, they will correct it. This promise reassures historians that the materials they find at these government sites have a very high likelihood of being credible and therefore useable as reference and instructional materials.

In the same document, the National Park Service assures us it complies with this directive in its promise to ensure quality in the materials it distributes. Its standard is that all information meets a high level of quality, with quality defined as "an encompassing term comprising utility, objectivity, and integrity" (www.nps.gov/policy/DOrders/11B-final.htm).

Solid, well-researched secondary sources also play a valuable role in historical study because, unlike tertiary sources, they are developed from serious study of primary sources. Such academic work shows the author did the necessary research and evaluation of materials to put together a cogent account. Secondary sources are a great starting point. They provide the overview you need to develop a working foundation of knowledge. These basics guide you toward understanding and make the daunting seem approachable. They lead you to the primary sources noted in the bibliography, giving you a head start on your own search for information and potential teaching materials.

The point to keep in mind is that secondary sources are still interpreters of primary sources, and the further you get from the original inside source, the more potential it has to become a game of telephone. When researched and used with integrity, though, secondary sources do an excellent job of making the content of hard-to-find primary materials available to us in one place. They have done the legwork for us and bring to light aspects of our history often hidden, glossed over, or neglected completely.

Desertion During the Civil War is an outstanding example of a quality secondary resource, this time on a less-than-complimentary aspect of the Civil War. Ella Lonn's 1928 book has stood the test of time as the bible on the subject of desertion. Her research revealed a problem of desertion so serious and growing so rapidly that on September 24, 1862, the Adjutant General's Office issued Government Order #140, which appointed a Provost Marshal General of the War Department and Special Provost Marshals for each state. The marshals served as the military police, charged with arresting deserters and those found to be disloyal or spies, and retrieving stolen property and keeping order (GO #140, 1862, Missouri State Archives).

Using *The War of the Rebellion: Official Records of the Union and Confederate Army*, some of which is now housed on the Cornell site, Making of

America, Lonn conducted an exhaustive study of the complicated issue of desertion by soldiers in the North and the South. Her focused study of all available records provides insight into the massive problem of desertion on both sides during the Civil War. She goes beyond one or a few sources to dig for and analyze any information she could find to get a truer account of what transpired, and why.

Lonn found the reasons for desertion to be many and the numbers of deserters staggering. In 1862, Union soldiers were deserting by the thousands (Lonn, p.153). Among the contributing factors, men deserted because they had little food and lacked basic necessities such as shoes, clothing, tents, and blankets; they were not paid regularly, sometimes waiting nine months or more for the pay they earned; they were homesick, or their families needed them; they were war-weary, injured, or ill, and they'd rather not fight anymore. On page 157, Lonn quotes Union General George McClellan as saying in disgust, "Not more than one tenth of the soldiers left behind sick ever returned to their company." His observation implies they died, became "invalids" in the Invalid Corps, were given a medical discharge, or simply chose to go elsewhere.

After considering all government and military records, officer and soldiers' correspondence, provost marshal records, and civil reports, and factoring in possible inaccuracies in statistics, Lonn made a conservative estimate that 200,000 individual Union and Confederate soldiers left their units, most never to return. In the eighty years since Lonn researched and wrote her book, no one has eclipsed her exhaustive assessment of desertion during the Civil War by reliability or thoroughness.

To the categories of primary and secondary sources, we can add another type called tertiary sources. Not all scholars and researchers distinguish between a secondary and tertiary source, since there is some overlap in their qualities. At times, the category to which a source belongs is a matter of individual or collective judgment. When they do stipulate a difference, they typically assign the label "tertiary" to what the University of Maryland Libraries defines as "information which is a distillation and collection of primary and secondary sources such as: Almanacs; Bibliographies (considered secondary by some); Chronologies; Dictionaries and Encyclopedias (also considered secondary); Directories; Fact books; Guidebooks; Indexes, abstracts, and bibliographies used to locate primary and secondary sources; Manuals; Textbooks (also considered secondary)" ("Primary, Secondary, and Tertiary Sources," n.d.).

These sources are attractive, especially for children or someone needing a crash course or a quick answer. They make it easy to locate information, read about it, and get enough knowledge to think we understand it. This false security gives meaning to the adage "a little information is a dangerous thing."

Looking at the plethora of types of material out there, we can understand why the study of history requires the scrutiny of a magnifying glass. It is a subjective minefield, the Wild West. As teachers, we have a special obligation to critically assess resources we use with students, recognize the sources' benefits and limitations, and make sure the sources pass the "high-quality test." Before we introduce a source to our students, we should have determined the kind of source it is, asked questions about the author, evaluated what was stated and what was implied, discovered the context in which it was written, and checked how it compares with other accounts.

This is the heart of historical study and document-based learning. As with everything we do, teachers should be exemplary role models for their students. We need to model this stringent process of historical study for our students.

Chapter 6:

Finding the Story

"There is properly no history, only biography."

—Ralph Waldo Emerson

Physical locations and other remnants of historical significance are everywhere. They are at roadside markers and historical sites, in old cemeteries, and in places we pass by every day. In the snippets of information on historical signs, in the names and ages of the buried, and in the homes, community buildings, businesses, and villages, we get a glimpse of the authentic story of the family life, the local customs, and the challenges the area faced.

Collecting and analyzing information about those who came before us is compelling. It speaks to that ingrained drive in us to understand and apply the lessons (concepts and essential understandings) we learn from others to our contemporary lives. Using primary and secondary historical resources and Bloom's hierarchy of thinking, we look for patterns, make connections, and draw conclusions. This process is personal. It allows us to piece together a story that makes sense to us.

When my elementary teachers and student teachers said they didn't like social studies—history in particular—I thought it unfortunate that they had not experienced history as something personally meaningful or had not been captivated by the stories. It made me realize that I was one of the lucky ones who had been caught in the web of history early in life.

In response to the negative feelings about history, I asked them if they ever thought of history as the stories of people and events in the context of time and place. I proposed that history is merely the collective lives of regular people and those who rose to a point of leadership, the choices they made, and how they handled blessings and adversity.

It is as simple as the elements that make a good book, play, or movie. Novels, documentaries, biographies and autobiographies, historical fiction, and true stories are compelling and touch something deep inside us. Successful stories resonate at an emotional level, stirring our curiosity to know more. They help us piggyback information and concepts as we continue to learn, providing the intellectual and emotional resources to better understand ourselves, each other, and the complexities of the world. Stories help us construct knowledge and concepts that are both elucidating and practical and that stay with us over time.

Stories enlighten and stimulate us. Their lure is especially strong when we know they are true. They take on new significance, and we have an instant respect for them.

I was serious when I told my preservice and classroom teachers that anything in history could be made interesting. Essentially, it depends on what

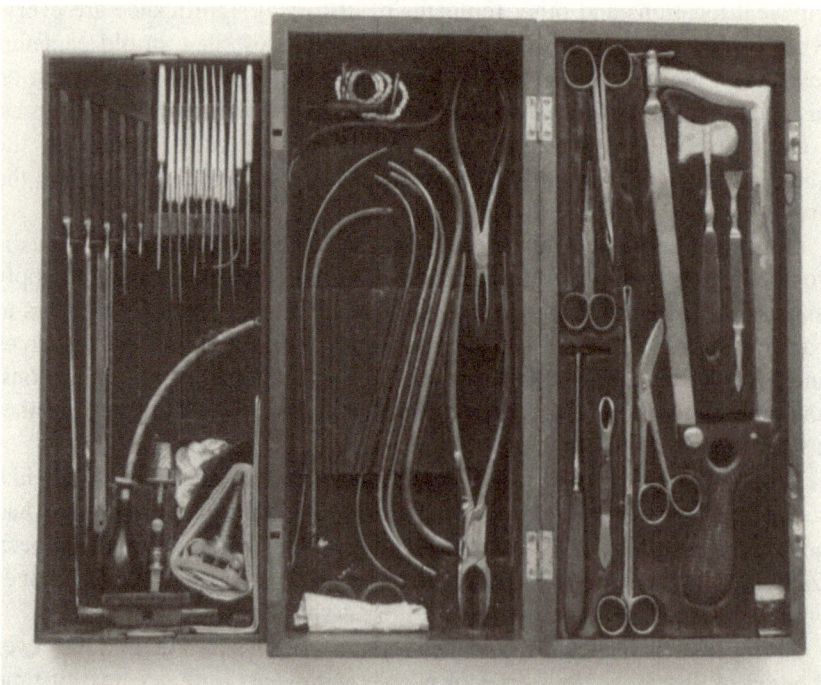

Photo 6.1 Authentic Snowden and Brothers Civil War surgeon's set. *Courtesy of Dr. Michael Echols, American Civil War Surgical Antiques.*

you share and how you share it. The trick is finding a hook to stimulate an immediate connection to present times and the learner. Then, it depends on building on that connection by delivering thought-provoking and engaging learning experiences for students. The stories and other intriguing tidbits that hook students do not need to be elaborate and are often found in the types of primary sources we mentioned: personal writings, diaries, letters, gravesites, autobiographies, official records, newspaper reports, artifacts, and personal objects. One simple instructional lesson where you read a letter or share pictures and objects can trigger and nurture a desire in your students to know the rest of the story.

The forces of human nature drive our behavior. People gossip and comment on what others do. They also congregate with those who are like themselves. People of any age get excited when they find out they have something in common with someone else. In classrooms, at work, in social situations, in blogs, and on personal websites, we seek connections when we seek to know: How old are you? Do you have children? Where did you grow up? Do you know so-and-so? What kind of work do you do? What do you like to do for fun? What movies and music do you like? What is your philosophy on life? And what are you passionate about?

We are also attracted by the intangible, yet very real, force we call chemistry. All of this exploring is a search for commonalities, a reaching out to make a meaningful connection with another person, to be part of something bigger than we are. If you find you don't have much in common with the person, or there is no chemistry, you lose interest.

The converse is also true. The more connections you find—the more you share core beliefs and values—the better the chances you will seek out and spend time with the person and want to know more of her story. It is the same with the study of history. Learners seek a connection with the content. If we find a connection, we are more likely to be motivated to stick with it and even go beyond the expected. It is the Velcro phenomenon. We have one half of the Velcro in our brain—memories, experiences, emotions, information, concepts—waiting to be stimulated, and the new information or idea is the other half, waiting to attach itself.

Whether you are a teacher, a student, or anyone else, for that matter, the brain loves stories and challenges. It does not like to be bored. Give us something we can personally relate to and our ears perk up. A wise teacher recognizes that this is a critical component of motivation and makes it happen for her students.

A major benefit to learning history through stories is the profound impact it has on our capacity to accept diversity. It compels us to consider points of view, circumstances, conflicting needs, and the way these factors affect

Photo 6.2 Title: "Migrant agricultural worker's family. Seven children without food. Mother aged thirty-two. Father is a native Californian. Nipomo, California" From Dorothea Lange's series "Migrant Mother" for the Farm Security Administration, 1936. *Courtesy Library of Congress, Prints & Photographs Division, FSA/OWI Collection, [reproduction number LC-USF34-T01–009095-C].*

choices. Teachers meet their obligations as educators when they challenge students to put themselves in the place of others and consider others' perspectives. Such a mental exercise trains the mind to be empathetic and analytical as a matter of habit and to think about people as individuals with decisions to make. It slows down the impulse to judge and dismiss, as it teaches us critical life lessons about the human condition. It gets us used to operating in the gray area; a little less comfortable, but quite stimulating.

This cognitive process has a valuable, practical outcome for society: it leads us to employ empathy and compassion in our daily lives and to consider the bigger picture of social justice. The result is more informed, fair-minded decision-making. If we are used to viewing the times and events through the eyes of all involved and exploring the motives behind an act or thought, we can draw more informed, nuanced, humane conclusions and elect leaders who see the complexity of the world.

As we mature and face increasingly complex issues, we are then prepared to consider the needs, wants, beliefs, ideas, and actions of others as we choose our own responses and behaviors. We are grounded. We witness and consider acts of bravery and savagery, humility and grandiosity, perseverance and capitulation, integrity and selfishness and everything in-between in the context of the story that surrounds them. We learn to apply our revelations to the person we want to be and the society we want to help create, and we are more inclined to take an active part in creating that society.

The stories of history give us an eye to the future. From the personal to the specific to the general, this is how we learn overarching concepts and essential truths about our collective human history. When we take a personal story approach to history, it helps us not lose the forest for the trees. We discover what lessons the trees can teach us about the forest.

Chapter 7:

What Do We Need to Teach?

"Let the science and research of the historian find the fact and let his imagination and art make clear its significance."

—George Trevelyan

What are the stories that both make history come alive and fit our instructional needs? Where do we find these resources? As we search for the best teaching approaches and materials to reach every student, we should be looking for a personal story or event that captures our interest and that also takes into account the developmental age and background of our students. This combination makes it likely that it will capture the students' interest as well as our own. We pass along our own enthusiasm for the topic and our own honed research and thinking skills, and we make them eager learners in the process. We have given them something substantial in which to engage.

Good teaching lives in the world of concepts:

1. A general notion or idea; conception.
2. An idea of something formed by mentally combining all its characteristics or particulars; a construct.
3. A directly conceived or intuited object of thought. (Dictionary.com)

Consider this "concept bank," a sampling of abstract thoughts and mental constructs: academic freedom, balance of powers, change, chauvinism, civic duty, civil rights, culture, community, compromise, conflict, cooperation, competition, conservation, courage, democracy, dignity, economy, empathy, enlightenment, equality, equity, fairness, free will, globalization, higher power, honesty, independence, integrity, interdependence, life cycle, motivation, nationalism, norms, oppression, patriotism, patterns, personal power, positional power, quality, racism, regionalism, relationships, respect, responsibility, revolution, sacrifice, security, selflessness, social justice, sustainability, trust, values, wants, and needs.

Concepts such as these provide the intuitive frame in which to make sense of specific information. From our own foundation of knowledge and deep understanding and a passion for the topic, we can successfully lead students through the core content of the curriculum and to a higher level of learning. As explained by H. Lynn Erickson in her book *Concept-Based Curriculum and Instruction*, we know enough about what we are teaching to help them formulate concepts and link them into statements of essential understandings such as these:

- Members of a *community* have a *responsibility* to work together to meet their *needs*.
- Healthy *relationships* require *empathy* and *compromise*.
- The *power* of a *government* can be used to create *fair* and socially *just laws*.

These big ideas, built on linked concepts, can be applied to the historical analysis of the next story or event students study or come across in real life.

Formulating this knowledge, understanding, and passion to teach historical subject matter with confidence and enthusiasm is quite doable. First, we need to find our own way to connect to the content and construct our own working knowledge base. Once we know the material and concepts and are inspired by the human stories, the world of history becomes a living entity for us, not some remote, dusty, daunting collection of facts and figures we have to teach.

In our formal study of history, we wisely follow this manageable cycle:

- We narrow the content to representative stories about a topic.
- We make a personal connection to the story and want to know more.
- We use these stories as a catalyst to ask questions and seek and comprehend information.
- We take this information and analyze it to construct broad, functional concepts and understandings.
- We use these concepts to think critically about future stories, information, and situations.

Who uses this cycle? Students, surely, and you, too! As you prepare to teach, you find yourself in the exciting role of learner—a learner with a lot of responsibility.

As this list infers, teaching is a continuous bombardment of decisions to make, and teachers need a defendable reason for whatever they do in their classrooms. It is a reflective profession where we are always evaluating what went well and what needs changing. Effective teachers self-evaluate and fine-tune as a matter of habit.

We must start by defining what we want students to know and be able to do as a result of our instruction. The question is, "Of all the things out there to teach, what is important enough for students to learn". The answer to this question typically comes from the learning standards, grade-level academic expectations, and assessments under which you are operating. These parameters help you define specific goals and objectives, choose appropriate materials, and develop lessons. When we make these judgments, we must be able to justify our choice of the instructional materials we use with students and be able to demonstrate that the content and materials pass this two-pronged test:

- The materials are age appropriate.
- The materials are relevant to the curriculum.

This test provides common-sense criteria for you to use as you choose the sources to teach history, and it preserves your right to teach points of view and information often overlooked due to an imposed, narrow agenda. Make a conscious effort to adhere to these criteria with an eye on your grade level, district, and state expectations as you design a course of study for your students, and you'll be on secure footing.

Outside expectations are a fact of life for teachers, and to our benefit, the current approach taken by learning standards toward history education is learning overarching, big ideas—the concepts and universal understandings. This is the basis of many state content-area performance standards created over the past twenty years, during the rise of the standards movement.

In 1994, the National Council on Social Studies (NCSS) developed national standards based on "Ten Thematic Strands in Social Studies," which they believe serve as a framework for exemplary social studies education (www.socialstudies.org/standards/curriculum).

Many state departments of education were busy doing the same. You can visit www.teachinghistory.org/teaching-materials/state-standards for a state-by-state search of social studies standards, and you can compare and contrast content and performance standards, concepts, and curriculum requirements. One commonality you'll likely find is that states all have a curricular strand on the history of their particular state. One contrast you will likely encounter is the specific people, issues, and events to be covered.

In their executive summary of the curriculum standards for social studies, the NCSS proclaims:

> For social studies to perform its mission of promoting civic competence, students must learn not only a body of knowledge, but how to think and how to be flexible in using many resources to resolve civic issues . . . these national curriculum standards for social studies represent educators' best thinking about what is needed to educate future citizens to meet that challenge. (Expectations of Excellence, n.d.)

What are we doing, if not preparing our graduates to be contributing members of society?

The New York State Education Department defines learning standards as "the knowledge, skills, and understandings that individuals habitually demonstrate over time as a consequence of instruction and experience." The standards, themselves, and the concepts inherent in the key ideas stay constant through the elementary, middle, and high school levels. What changes is the depth and breadth of the instruction, the content, the materials used, the expectations, and the assessments. In New York, students at all levels will:

> Use a variety of intellectual skills to demonstrate their understanding of major ideas, eras, themes, developments, and turning points in the history of the United States and New York.
>
> Key Idea 1: The study of New York State and United States history requires an analysis of the development of American culture, its diversity and multicultural context, and the ways people are unified by many values, practices, and traditions. (NYSED, 1996)

Looking at the Iowa State Standards for Social Studies, you find that, as in New York, there is a running thread of essential understandings throughout the grades. The understandings are identified as enduring universal principles that apply to everyone. What changes is the sophistication of what we expect from students at varying developmental levels. Both Iowa and New York ask their students to use and value primary and secondary sources and to be critical evaluators of information. Iowa State Standards:

> For Grades K–2
> Understand cause and effect relationships and other historical thinking skills in order to interpret events and issues.
>
> History can provide opportunities for students to develop analysis and critical reasoning skills. Understanding cause and effect relationships is the foundation of historical analysis. Students use critical thinking skills to question and explore historical events and issues.

For Grades 6–8
Understand cause and effect relationships and other historical thinking skills in order to interpret events and issues.
Some of the historical thinking skills include consideration of multiple perspectives, analysis of historical narrative, and construction of historical hypotheses. By interpreting and analyzing the decisions of past societies, students gain the ability to evaluate current events, issues, and decisions. (Iowa Core, Iowa Department of Education)

With the scope, sequence, and expected student outcomes of the curriculum now typically prescribed by the district or state, teachers no longer get to avoid teaching what they don't like or choose what they teach according to what interests them or their students. At the least, they cannot do this without it legitimately fitting into the context of the curriculum and meeting the standardized curricular expectations and benchmarks for student performance.

Standards provide direction. With standards in place, you can focus on the stories and primary and secondary resources. Your choice of source material need not deviate from the content and skills prescribed by the formal curriculum you are required to teach. Instead, the standards give you flexibility in choosing the materials and approaches you can use to lead your students to these prescribed competencies.

This is where your academic freedom and creativity lie. You end at the same place, but in getting there, your students have been more personally motivated and engaged. Subsequently, they emerge as better thinkers with a truer understanding of events than those who worked with a historical skeleton of facts and figures. Such a concept-driven experience with history stays with you and your students long after the formal instruction is over. As the NYSED definition of "learning standard" tells us, what you know and can do should be habitually demonstrated over time.

To approach the curriculum in this conceptual way, teachers need to define exactly what drives their teaching. State what you want them to internalize. You have now identified your goals, the ultimate conceptual understandings that are of most importance. Until you go through this process, you will not be able to clearly focus your instruction on anything more than the basic knowledge and comprehension levels from which we want to move away.

Accomplishing this takes motivation and creative thinking on the teacher's part. It is critical that teachers recognize that they have the professional flexibility and opportunity to make decisions about:

- How we approach the content—Our angle.
- The materials we use.
- Ways we involve the students.

- Where we place the emphasis.
- What we use to assess and evaluate student learning.

Then, as suggested in "Putting Historical Thinking Skills to Work" (nchs.ucla.edu/standards/thinking5-12-6.html), we ask students to: compare, reconstruct, hypothesize, marshal evidence, interrogate, differentiate, and challenge.

When we look at it this way, we do have a good amount of freedom, especially when we consider this latitude to make these decisions exists even in the climate of high-stakes standardized testing and stringent across-the-board benchmarks and graduation requirements.

Chapter 8:

Teachers, the Natural Collectors

"What you seek, exists within you. Every resource you need is available to you."

—Marcia Wieder

With this academic freedom comes the responsibility of familiarity and mastery acquired through thorough preparation and hard work. If history is the collective result of millions of individual stories, we must get down to the business of finding the specific materials that suit our instructional needs.

We've defined our curricular and instructional goals, which in turn gave us the direction and parameters for the materials we chose. Finding appropriate stories that inspire and intrigue is a matter of researching what is out there; there is plenty of material waiting to be brought to life. As we discussed previously, search your topic on the Internet and consult websites for teachers. Read everything you can find, and ask your colleagues what they already have. They are an easily accessible and rich resource and would likely want to join you in this educational pursuit.

A piece of personal writing, an official document, a newspaper article, or a political cartoon from the past serve as excellent ways to hook your students' interest in the broad topic. Remember the forest and the trees: start with the personal, apply to the specific, and conclude with the universal.

In addition to written sources, history is also brought to life through artifacts of the times. Objects that students can look at or hold have great motivational power and the ability to raise good questions, trigger predictions, and inspire artistic creativity. Look around you. Objects have their own stories to tell.

Teachers are collectors. We find a use for everything! When I started my life as a teacher, my vacations and Saturday mornings at garage sales took on a new focus. Wherever I went, I saw potential in objects and books that I could use in my classroom. My teaching collections grew, and my camera became a teaching tool. When visiting California, I took pictures of Father Serra's sparse quarters in the Spanish Mission at San Diego. When at Little Bighorn in Montana, I collected postcards of photographs and quotes of the Lakota Indian leaders, and I took pictures of the landscape where General Custer had his last stand. When at a small Mohegan Indian Museum in Connecticut, I spoke with a Native American docent who explained how pemmican was made and carried, and I took home a few arrowheads.

While the objects I collected on my trips were not originals, if they were a direct copy or representative reproduction, they had a legitimate use as a teaching tool. Such objects are interesting and make history more tangible and approachable. They are the jumping-off place, the catalyst for questions and immersion into a topic of study. A small model of a pyramid from Egypt that students can hold and observe helps them develop a conceptual understanding of a pyramid that no picture or description can, and it gets them to start asking questions.

In her article, "Teaching History Through Material Culture," included in the 1994 journal *Illinois History Teacher,* Janice Tauer Wass talks about such artifacts and objects as "material culture" and offers teachers curricular suggestions for teaching with artifacts. She defines material culture as "the physical evidence of human experience. It includes the vast numbers of objects that people use in every aspect of their lives, everything from buttons, tools, ceramics, and furniture to houses, roads, and cities" (Wass, 1994, para. 1).

When planning a unit, why not look at what you already have of instructional value at home or at school? Among my collection of family memorabilia and other "interesting" things from the past is a gently-yellowed business card circa 1910 for Catherine, my grandmother-in-law. The card says "fashionable dressmaker."

When she gave it to me, my first reaction was surprise—surprise that a woman living in the early 1900s would have had a business card. This one small memento jumpstarted the story of how she lost her mother at a young age, ran away from home at age thirteen, lived in a boarding house with a generous, caring family, and found a livelihood. At a time when women had few legal and political rights, Kitty, a quiet, retiring person by nature, used her personal power to orchestrate her own independence, her own future. Somehow, she had learned to sew and found she had a talent for it, a talent that could earn her a living.

Teachers, the Natural Collectors 57

Photo 8.1   Kitty's memorabilia. *Author's collection.*

Her story can be the catalyst for a host of topics of study and concept building, such as through this introductory activity that follows.

Collect enough business cards for each student to have one. Pass them out, and brainstorm a list of common characteristics of business cards and the information they include—name, profession/title, company/organization, physical location, email address, land and cell phone numbers, fax number, website—and what they look like—size, shape, color of the card and design elements, graphics, photographs, font style, slogans, and logo. One student has Kitty's card, and it stands out dramatically from the others. Through this simple learning activity that engages every student, you have hooked your students and started your course of study with a bang. The business card and tale of Kitty's early life leads to the bigger issues of the time.

With interest in Kitty's story now piqued, let students work together to predict the time period of the card. Ask them to defend their predictions. Have them discuss how clothes are made now and why Kitty might have been called a "fashionable dressmaker." Discuss how Kitty was a highly skilled dressmaker with well-to-do customers that came to the dress shop where she worked, looking for her to create custom dresses and elaborate and unique hats. We can look at a picture of a hat and dress she made for herself for an outing with her boarding-room friends. This was before 1915, when she married and took on the more traditional female role of homemaker and mother in the first quarter of twentieth-century America.

In stark contrast, during this time in history, many women sewed in hot, cramped, stuffy sweatshops amidst rows and rows of tables, noisy and dangerous sewing machines, and piles of scrap material. They did this for long hours and little money, six days a week.

Kitty's desirable situation was a product of both her character and her personal circumstances. Unlike most of the women relegated to sweatshops who were from Italy and Eastern Europe, with little or no English skills and meager resources, she was not a recent immigrant. She had suffered her own personal adversities, yet she was privileged by her heritage, race, ethnicity, and the story into which she was born. While not wealthy when they came to America, her Northern European ancestors either already spoke English, or they had learned the language generations ago. By the time Kitty joined the story, they had been assimilated into the American culture and were financially stable.

She was not famous, but Kitty lived under society's restrictive expectations for women and had a story to tell. Through these artifacts, we get a sense of her life and circumstances, and we can put a personal face to a pre-suffrage American woman.

The story of Kitty and the themes of women's rights, working conditions, industrialization of cities, and labor unions draw us to the infamous New York City Triangle Shirtwaist Factory Fire of 1911. Cornell University's "The Triangle Factory Fire" site is rich with primary resources, including oral histories, diaries, photographs of the fire, and transcripts from the manslaughter trial of the owners of the Triangle Shirtwaist Company. These personal accounts and trial transcripts tell a gripping story with the intrigue of a novel ("The Triangle Factory Fire," n.d.).

Everyone wore shirtwaists in the early 1900s. These prim women's blouses, worn with a skirt, were cut and sewn by laborers, hour upon hour, with the material remnants left in huge scrap piles each day to be sold to rag collectors. One Saturday evening, on March 25, 1911, at quitting time, in typical deplorable sweatshop conditions, eight, nine, and ten stories up, a fire broke out on the eighth floor of the Asch Building in a pile of those material scraps.

It was a flash fire, one that quickly spread over the eighth floor of the sweatshop, and within three minutes, to the ones above. Smoke billowed in through the windows, sending hundreds of workers on the ninth floor, almost all women, rushing first to the fire escape, only to find it twisted and collapsed from the heat, and then to the elevator. The elevator operator made

Photo 8.2 "The Locked Door" political cartoon reacting to the Triangle Factory Fire. *Courtesy of the International Ladies Garment Workers Union Archives, Kheel Center, Cornell University.*

a few courageous trips up and down to rescue some of the workers. When he and the elevator could no longer sustain the heat and smoke, he stopped. In desperation, some jumped down the open elevator shaft, falling to their deaths.

Things were happening very fast. A crowd gathered at the only usable exit, a door located on the other side of the workroom, behind wooden partitions.

But it wasn't usable. It was locked. Flames licked close as they tried in vain to open the door to the stairs, a door that opened in, not out. Above and below them, workers were fleeing down these stairs or heading to the roof. Those on the ninth floor pulled on the knob, screaming and banging on the door for someone to open it. There was now no way left to escape the inferno except by the windows.

Within minutes of the fire breaking out, the street became a morgue. It was littered with the bodies of those who jumped from nine floors up to the concrete below, witnessed by bystanders, unable to do anything but watch in horror or try to break their fall with useless fire nets.

When it was over and all the bodies were found, one hundred forty-six people had died on March 25, 1911, the vast majority young immigrant girls in their teens and early twenties who worked long, tedious hours, with little fresh air and poor light, for low wages, in what turned out to be a firetrap.

The March 26, 1911, *New York Times* reported it this way:

> 141 Men and Girls Die in Waist Factory Fire; Trapped High Up in Washington Place Building; Street Strewn with Bodies; Piles of Dead Inside
>
> Three stories of a ten-floor building at the corner of Greene Street and Washington Place were burned yesterday, and while the fire was going on 141 young men and women at least 125 of them mere girls were burned to death or killed by jumping to the pavement below. (As cited in "The Triangle Factory Fire," n.d.)

We get a deeper understanding of the situation from an investigative article, "Fire and the Skyscraper," by Arthur E. McFarlane, published in the May 1911 issue of *McClure's Magazine* (McFarlane, 1911, pp. 455–482). His comprehensive look at the history of manufacturing and labor disputes in early nineteenth-century New York City enlightens the reader about the conditions that led to the Triangle Factory fire and the loss of so many lives. As is often the case with tragedies, the fire became a rallying cry. It intensified the already mounting anger over working conditions, and fueled support for organized unions and regulations. The deaths of the 146 workers resulted in the passage of thirty-six new labor laws for the factory workers of New York.

All that was written and has been said about the Triangle Factory fire—eye-witness testimony, trial transcripts, fire department reports, newspaper articles, investigations, memoirs of survivors, diaries—tell the story of a tragedy that could and should have been avoided:

- The building was ten stories high, a loft style, never built with a manufacturing purpose in mind.
- The rooms were overcrowded with tables, with some pushed up against the windows.
- Chairs at the tables were so close that they butted together as the women worked back-to-back.
- Material scraps had not been picked up by the scrap company in months.
- Oil from the machines soaked the wood floor and the cloth scraps.
- There was no fire emergency escape plan.
- The fire department hoses could only reach as high as the seventh story.
- The extension ladders could only reach the sixth floor.
- The fire escape melted, the elevator buckled, and flames were sucked through the open windows of the floors above.
- The stairway door on the Washington Street side was locked to force workers to file slowly down a three-foot-wide staircase on the Green Street side

of the building. It was so narrow they had to descend one at a time, providing the guard ample time to look in each of their bags for stolen scrap material. (McFarlane, Arthur E., 1911, May)

Look where this small business card led us! With so simple an artifact, students are able to connect the story of a person who was born in 1894 with the universal elements of greed and power, the plight of women, minorities, laborers, and the poor. We can capitalize on the interest generated by her story to segue beautifully into pivotal points in American history, like the story of the Triangle Shirtwaist Fire or to an exploration of:

- America in the early twentieth century, with industrialization and the growth of cities, immigration, and concerns about working conditions and labor laws.
- What the world was like geopolitically before and after World War I.
- The seventy-two-year struggle for women's suffrage that started in 1848 in Seneca Falls, New York, and ended in 1920 when Congress and the states amended the U.S. Constitution to give women the right to vote (it was ratified by a one-vote margin in the Tennessee state legislature, a remarkable story in itself).
- The 1919 national prohibition of the manufacture, sale, and transportation of intoxicating liquors, the carefree "lost generation" of the roaring twenties of F. Scott Fitzgerald, and the rise of organized crime and gangsters.
- Life in the 1930s when the sudden 1929 crash of the stock market plunged the country into the Great Depression, with bread lines and unemployment as high as 25 percent.
- Franklin Delano Roosevelt's New Deal of government programs to put Americans to work and provide home relief, social security, and the lasting effect of Roosevelt's Works Progress Administration projects on American art and architecture.

Looking at this list, we discover so many parallels to contemporary life—war, economic depression and unemployment, legalization of drugs, drunk driving, illegal immigration, social and political equity, universal health care, human trafficking and forced labor, the widening division between the haves and the have-nots, and the struggle between those who believe government is responsible for the well-being of its citizens and those who think less government is better government. These topics touch on economics, politics, law, government, civics, art, and human rights, all aspects of the rich social studies curriculum.

Photo 8.3 Theater poster for "Battle hymn," a play about John Brown of Harpers Ferry, Federal Theatre Project 1936–41. *Courtesy of the Library of Congress, Prints and Photographs Division, WPA Poster Collection, [reproduction number LC-USZC2–5373 DLC]*

Kitty's life story—her history—is interesting and telling in itself, but its main value is the entré it provides into new areas of study for us and for our students. This combination of artifacts and anecdotes leads students to the knowledge base and essential understandings asked of them by the formal curriculum. Viewing them in a new light—as useful little slices of history waiting to spark interest—we might just find such simple, yet inspirational and intriguing, anecdotes and artifacts in our own families.

Primary materials beg us to ask questions and speculate. One of my school districts knew the power objects had to bring history alive. Someone had the foresight to capitalize on the many ethnic groups drawn to the area by the city's two universities. They created cultural discovery boxes that could be borrowed from a central location. Each box contained authentic clothing, pieces of art, and other objects from that particular ethnic group or country, along with explanations of the items.

We would sit in a circle, open the box, and carefully and thoughtfully take out each item and pass it around. The students learned to be respectful of the materials and thoughtful in their inspection and questions. They knew the expectation was no laughing at what was unfamiliar and different appearing or sounding from what we were accustomed. The students' observations spurred them to want to know more about the culture, and along the way, they learned to appreciate the diversity of the world's people. It was similar to the "personality boxes" of artifacts students brought in at the beginning of each school year to introduce themselves to their teacher and classmates.

These boxes were a wonderful jumping-off point for units of study—that catalyst we mentioned. Every classroom, regardless of the age of the students, would benefit from similar boxes of artifacts, objects, and art, where teachers, families, and the public could pool their resources to open up new worlds for their children. Imagine the motivational power of a box containing nineteenth century household tools, children's books and toys from various cultures, samples of different written alphabets and writing implements, or one of clothing in the materials and array of styles found in different parts of the world.

The Gettysburg National Historic Park recognizes the power of tangibles as learning tools. It offers for loan to classrooms "The Life of the Civil War Soldier," traveling trunks filled with authentic reproductions of the clothing soldiers wore, relevant photographs, things they used to pass the time, military objects, and a teacher's guide. The best part? Students may handle the materials. Now that's what students and teachers call motivating!

Chapter 9:

Oral Traditions—Tell me about . . .

"There is no history, only histories."

—Karl Popper

Primary resources can also be oral histories collected from people in general, or from those living at a specific time, in a specific place, or who experienced a specific event. They are typically written down or recorded by others as a permanent record of their firsthand perspective. They record what happened so it can never be forgotten.

Oral histories take the imperative, "Let me tell you a story," and switch it around to the request, "Please tell me about . . . ." Here, the listener expresses interest by making the request. People are most often happy to cooperate when given the opportunity to share their life with an enthusiastic listener. It is very affirming to think you have something valuable to share, and the reality is we all do.

"I remember being in court every day," Sylvia Mendez says to her sister, Sandra Mendez Duran in their Story Corps interview. They were talking about *Mendez v. Westminster*, their parents' 1945 groundbreaking court case against the LA area school district that practiced segregation of Mexican and white students. You and your students can listen to the interview at storycorps.org/?s=mendez and let it initiate a spirited discussion of racial and ethnic concerns, then and now.

This piece is from Story Corps, a project where people interview others important to them, listening respectfully to what they have to say. It is different from a typical interview because the interviewer and the interviewee know each other well. These conversations give an eyewitness, personal account of life at a point in time. The interviewer asks the person to tell about some aspect of his or her life. Each conversation is recorded and preserved at the American Folklife Center at the Library of Congress and made available to the public. They are also heard regularly on National Public Radio stations.

Teachers and students can visit the Story Corps website (storycorps.org), browse through an index of categories, and listen to a large selection of the more than 50,000 stories preserved for posterity. They even explain how you can record a conversation with someone important in your life to add to the 50,000 (Story Corps: The Conversation of a Lifeline, n.d.).

Densho means, "to pass on to the next generation." To teach history from the perspective of personal experience, and to archive what really happened, the Densho project of Seattle has conducted hundreds of hours of interviews with Japanese Americans forcibly removed by the U.S. government from their West Coast homes during World War II. In what the government saw as a matter of national security after Pearl Harbor, over 100,000 Japanese-American men, women, and children were uprooted and transported against their will to be incarcerated in physically isolated, crowded, fenced-in internment camps, with armed guards to keep them there. You can visit the Densho website to listen to some of their 800 hours of interviews, read their compelling personal stories, and look at visual histories of Japanese Americans and others affected by the World War II incarceration (Densho: The Japanese American Legacy Site, www.densho.org).

The Manzanar National Historic Site, which sits in the Owens Valley at the foothills of the Sierra Nevada Mountains of California, stands as witness of such an internment camp. Located some 120 miles west of Death Valley National Park, Manzanar sits 4,000 feet above sea level and experiences dry, hot summers and cold winters.

The site preserves the remnants of the Japanese American incarceration camp established there in 1942. Visit their website or, better yet, visit in person. The interpretive center, housed in the former camp high school, the guard tower, the cemetery, and the remnants of building foundations, orchards, and rock gardens will have a lasting impact on you. A related book, *Farewell to Manzanar,* by Jeanne Wakatsuki and her husband, James D. Houston, is a compelling memoir of Wakatsuki's experience as a young girl in the Manzanar camp that you and older students would enjoy (www.nps.gov/manz/index.htm).

Other storytelling ventures like the California Council for the Humanities *Communities Speak, California Documentary Project,* and *California Story Fund* engage people in various communities to speak to those they do not know. They tell each other about their lives, their experiences, and

Photo 9.1 Japanese-American Internment Camp Cemetery Memorial with Sierra Nevada Mountains in background, Manzanar National Historic Site, Owens Valley, California. *Author's collection.*

their perspectives, something they would typically discuss only with close family and friends. Their mission statement makes their purpose clear: "The California Council for the Humanities is to connect Californians to ideas and one another in order to understand our shared heritage and diverse cultures, inspire civic participation, and shape our future" (www.calhum.org/about/about_mission.htm).

Executive Director Jim Quay in the CCH organization's Spring 2003 newsletter says it works: "What we have found is that when people tell their stories and other people listen, a trust is created that can change community dynamics" (Quay, 2003, p.1).

Teachers can harness and use this power in their classrooms. Ask your students to create their own primary sources from which they and others can benefit by having them interview people who lived at a certain time or place. They will learn important life lessons: that everyone has a story, that firsthand accounts have a powerful impact, and that it is difficult to hurt or be disdainful of those whose stories you know. Stories build understanding and compassion, as well as provide information and perspective.

Now that we are inspired by the power of a story told by authentic primary materials, knowledgeable of what a standard-driven curriculum requires we teach, aware of the kinds of materials available, where to find these materials, and how to assess their value, we are ready to teach our students. Or are we?

Chapter 10:

Making It Formal and Losing the Spirit

"History is reading all that you can as fast as you can and—remembering as much as you can."

—Lynn Berleffi Darr

Remember back to the first question I asked you about your memories. What did "Let me tell you a story" conjure up for you? What did you answer? Have you always liked a good story?

If you are like most people, the answer is yes. It is human nature. Stories about family and friends and the intrigue these stories create fuel the intensity of personal relationships. Popular culture is steeped in a desire to hear the details of the lives of the famous and infamous. In spite of ourselves, we are often mesmerized by the ins and outs of the doings of others, including absolute strangers we first hear about in the news.

Over all others, the power of primary resources and the stories they tell touch us emotionally and challenge us intellectually. The preference is clear when we weigh the value of memorizing loosely connected information at a defined point in time (grade level), a certain place (classroom), or for a limited purpose (a test) with that of experiencing human history.

Later on in the book, in the tale of my Civil War soldier who was at the Battle of Shiloh mentioned in the army field report, and in the subject of Private Lougheed's letter to his wife, Jennie, you experience how poignant and lasting an impression authentic voices from the past can have and how long their stories can stay with us.

They stay with us because they represent the gamut of human experience, and we are curious about how other people live. In its most pure state, our curiosity makes us look critically at ourselves and challenge our own thinking. We reflect as we compare ourselves to others, asking, "What kind a person would do that? Did he do the right thing? What would I do if I were in that situation? Do I agree with the choices made?" We do this questioning all the time, starting as children.

Children are socialized through stories and by observing and modeling after others. Life is a flow of personal connections, cause and effect, and the behaviors we choose. Children are going through this very human developmental learning process when formal schooling comes along; some might say when it comes along and interferes. From our childhood world of free-flowing spontaneous play, fanciful stories, and free choice, we are plunked down in a classroom where someone else determines what we must learn, when we learn it, how we learn it, and when we are done learning it. It is no secret that, especially when it comes to content area subjects, formal education can siphon off our natural curiosity to explore and learn. Nowhere is this more evident and avoidable than when we are formally taught history.

An inordinate amount of history instruction is spent memorizing dates, names, places, and pieces of disconnected information while taking pages of notes to help students remember all of it so they can study for the test. Students are too often presented information that is predigested in tertiary sources, those history textbooks and other commercially prepared instructional materials targeted specifically at the lucrative classroom market. The goal is often shallow: These are the main ideas and supporting details. Now, remember the information for one specific moment in time—when you are formally tested on it—and let's move on.

This is what bland, surface-level, presweetened, predigested textbook accounts do to our students. And students show us they are locked into this pattern when they ask, "Is that important? Should we write it down? Will it be on the test? What chapters should we study?" Afterwards, it all slips from their memories through irrelevance and disuse. Did they ever really learn it? Not if learning means committing information to the long-term memory for use in the future. Absent a personal meaning, it wasn't important enough for them to learn it, and they didn't.

Once we get to the intermediate grades and to middle and high school, social studies is usually an unwieldy curriculum teachers and students must churn through at a quick pace. There is an understandable, driving force behind this practice: the need to cover material, to prepare students to do well on exit exams and standardized tests, to help students meet graduation requirements, and to perform well on national assessments. There is even the duress of our salaries being dependent on how well our students do on these tests. At the expense of personalizing history with primary materials and constructing our own knowledge and understanding, in two or three weeks, we cover whole civilizations.

- Before Halloween we should be done with Mesopotamia.
- By Thanksgiving finish up Ancient Egypt.
- Cover Ancient Greece in the short month of December.
- Be ready to start Rome when we return in January.

A pervasive mantra reminding us not to get behind or be sidetracked drives the curriculum and our teaching style, not the needs of the student or what we know is best practice. The date of the test is never far from our thoughts. We must keep plugging along to stay on schedule with the rest of our grade level teachers, teachers in the other schools in our district, and even other history teachers around the state, and make-believe that snow days, assemblies, holidays, and student questions don't happen.

One way history is typically represented is through a historical timeline. It organizes history chronologically and provides us with a graphic frame of reference; it is a helpful instructional tool. We can't stop there. We need to explore what it all means. The milestones noted might all sound interesting, but they have limited meaning without our digging deeper to find context and develop perspective. As with any author, the creator of the timeline—a tertiary source—makes the decision about what to include and what to omit.

Consider this example I put together:

Timeline of the History of Women's Rights in America.
1789   U.S. Constitution ratified and goes into effect.
1830   My Civil War soldier, Van, is born.
1848   First Women's Rights Convention held in Seneca Falls, New York.
1861   The American Civil War begins—fight for women's rights on hold.
1865   Civil War ends, Reconstruction begins.
1868   Fourteenth Amendment to the U.S. Constitution gives all male citizens the right to vote.
1884   My Italian grandparents are born.
1893   New Zealand first country to give women right to vote.
1895   My three-year-old grandfather emigrates from Germany to New York City.
1903   National Women's Trade Union established for better working conditions.
1917   Russia gives women right to vote.
1919   My father is born.
1920   Nineteenth Amendment gives U.S. women right to vote.

1921 My mother is born.
1923 Equal Rights Amendment first proposed to Congress.
1940–45 World War II propaganda campaign to get women to work in typically male jobs.
1951 I'm born.
1956 Number of women in the work force up from 8.5 million in 1947 to almost 13 million.
1959 American Medical Association sanctions birth control for the first time.
1960 FDA approves birth-control pill.
1963 President's "Commission on Status of Women" finds women discriminated against in almost all aspects of U.S. life.
1964 Title VII Civil Rights Act prohibits discrimination in employment by race or gender.
1970 Congress approves the Equal Rights Amendment, first step toward adoption.
1972 ERA sent to states for ratification; Title IX becomes law.
1973 *Roe v. Wade* upheld by U.S. Supreme Court.
1976 Nebraska adopts the first law making it illegal for a husband to rape his wife.
1977 My son is born.
1979 My daughter is born.
1986 Supreme Court rules sexual harassment on the job is sex discrimination.
1992 American Association of University Women release their report, "How Schools Shortchange Girls."
1993 Violence Against Women Act passes.
1994 Congress adopts Gender Equity in Education Act.
2001 American Association of University Women release *Beyond the "Gender Wars": A Conversation about Girls, Boys, and Education.*
2009 Lilly Ledbetter Fair Pay Restoration Act passed.
2010 ERA not yet ratified by a three-fourths majority of U.S. states.

Filled with interesting tidbits, this women's rights timeline might make us want to know more about what happened and why. Inserting milestones of my life made it more relevant to me and would do the same for you and your students. It put my life into context. Yet, it is apparent that a historical timeline does not tell the story of history, the same as a personal timeline would not tell the story of your life. As it stands, it is a lifeless organizational construct, a chronology, helpful but with limited meaning, dwelling at the bottom level of the thinking-skills taxonomy. What it does provide is a relational picture, historical context that helps us deconstruct the story we've been told. Do research, annotate it with primary and secondary sources, and draw connections between events to develop concepts and essential understandings, and you breathe life into the timeline of history.

With history tied too tightly to dates and factoids, it is understandable why so many teachers said they hated social studies and didn't want to teach it. History-phobic teachers are a product of their past just as I am a product of mine. Their prior school experiences ruined history for them. They equate social studies with history and history with facts upon facts with little relevance, facts that they now must be facile with so they can teach them to their students. This misconception presents history as a daunting, distasteful discipline to teach; a fact-based, rapid-fire curriculum bled dry of its humanity.

Teachers find themselves faced with their nemesis, and understandably, the thought scares them. They don't know a way to teach it other than the way they were taught themselves. They have no intrinsic feel for history, derive no pleasure from it, and don't know much about it. They have never learned to love history or to approach it with an intellectual curiosity, and this has a tremendous impact on quality of instruction.

How can you teach what you don't like? Try it. It either falls flat or a miracle occurs, and in spite of yourself, you get inspired and become inspiring. Even college education classes focused on the pedagogy of teaching social studies cannot take root if the soon-to-be teacher still has the internal message that history is a boring, lifeless, tedious subject. Boredom is just as contagious as enthusiasm. Whether we like or dislike the subject matter shows in our teaching.

Elizabeth Green's March 7, 2010, *New York Times Magazine* article, "Can Good Teaching be Learned?" seeks to identify the elusive qualities that make a good teacher, a question we've been asking forever. Two qualities surfaced: excellent classroom-management skills and a deep knowledge of the content and how to teach it (Green, 2010).

Accepting that making history come alive is a product of your attitudes, content knowledge, teaching skills, and your own personal engagement puts the responsibility on your shoulders. An energetic, knowledgeable teacher can make anything interesting, while an unenthusiastic or ill-prepared teacher can take what could be fascinating and complex and reduce it to a lackluster curriculum. I've seen both scenarios over and over. In the classroom, students' natural love of stories and making connections—the things that could engage them in the content—are either nurtured or squandered.

Something has to change for these teachers. Unless students are motivated by an intrinsic passion (possibly fueled by family trips, a history buff at home, or a great teacher in their past), the formal study of history fails and succeeds on the quality of the presentation and exposure. Along the line of

"If you build it, they will come," the famous line from *Field of Dreams*—if we love what we teach and teach it well, they will love it, too.

So, how do we get there? Again, Bruner makes the point, "Rather than just retaining knowledge and facts, they go beyond them to use their imaginations to think about other outcomes . . . This helps them to think about facing the future, and it stimulates the teacher too" (Crace, 2007, para. 3).

Chapter 11:

Getting Inspired So You Can Inspire

"There are three things to remember when teaching: know your stuff; know whom you are stuffing; and then stuff them elegantly."

—Lola May

Interest. Motivation. Curiosity. When it comes to teaching history, how do teachers develop a fascination that turns into inspirational teaching? They do this by getting hooked themselves and continually saying, "That's interesting," and, "I wonder," searching for answers, and by seeing the bigger picture where all the social sciences and humanities intersect.

One of the elements of a good teacher Greene identified is an authentic enthusiasm about the content. These teachers approach it like a puzzle or a mystery and put together the story! The often-used adage that teachers need to be life-long learners is at the crux of good teaching and a satisfying career. Your journey to learn the content forms a natural path to inspired teaching (cause) and authentic student learning (effect). If you are one of those who say you don't like social studies, your task is to convince yourself otherwise. If you are lucky to be one who enjoys history, there are many ways to expand your understandings and make your teaching more intellectually challenging and memorable.

Discover the relevance of historical events to your life now. Consider the rich story inherent in the passage of the Eighteenth Amendment to the U.S. Constitution, ratified on January 16, 1919, prohibiting the manufacture, sale, and transportation of alcohol anywhere in the United States, and the 1933 Twenty-first Amendment, repealing the Eighteenth. Why would Congress take such a drastic step in the first place, and why did it change its mind fourteen years later? What was going on in society at those times?

The story of prohibition is relevant today. One legacy of the prohibition experiment is America's entrenched institution of organized crime, still a major destructive force in our society, maybe even in our own lives. The correlation of alcohol abuse to violent crime and incarceration, which fueled the temperance movement in the early 1900s, is a serious present-day ill. Alcohol abuse was even a problem with the troops during the Civil War, as U.S. General George McClelland expressed in February 1862: "No one evil obstructs this army as the degrading vice of drunkenness. It is the cause of, by far, the greater part of the disorders which are examined by court martial" (Smoking and Drinking, Camp Life Civil War Collections, n.d.). The concepts are timeless; only the specific circumstances change, and we might find there are parallels between time periods.

Intriguing materials and healthy relationships are fundamental factors in teaching success. Teachers define the relationship they have with their students through the choices they make, which is a major factor in their ability to manage the classroom and teach effectively. The learning environment should inspire students. With a positive classroom climate and a solid content background, you are prepared to make good decisions about the aspects of the curriculum over which you have some control: classroom expectations, behavioral norms, instructional strategies, use of time, choice of materials, lesson design, learning experiences, and types of assessments (at least some of them). This means de-emphasizing the trivia that ruins social studies for students and for the teachers who must teach it.

Engaged, motivated, respected students behave better, and you can teach them more effectively. They recognize and appreciate it when a teacher goes out of her way to make learning fun and challenging. The relationship is summed up by this simple equation: Positive relationships + engaging teaching = fewer discipline problems + increased learning.

K–12 teachers do not need to know the content to the same level as a college professor who specializes in the topic. They do need to know substantially more than the layperson and their students. There is no escaping the fact that it requires a lot of effort to learn the subject matter to a point of deep understanding. This could easily seem overwhelming at first, especially for new teachers who are often just "a chapter" ahead of their students.

Build a frame of reference using select tertiary sources. For an introduction, Google your topic, and explore the wealth of information available. Scan encyclopedia entries, and go to the school library to read children's and young adult books with an eye out for names, events, and keywords. This gives you direction for further research.

Take this basis and read articles and conduct research on the Internet. Visit museums and historic sites virtually or in person. Scour teaching websites and read lesson plans on your topic. The National History Education Clearinghouse (www.teachinghistory.org) is an excellent source of lesson plans with related primary documents, and it includes a useful planning rubric. Use this information to narrow your search to tales of people who lived during the times, and read related books and biographies, and watch films and documentaries. Look in your own family and at your own artifacts, all the while looking for themes, patterns, and concepts. Listen to audio recordings and watch news clips. Read "A Systematic Approach to Improve Students' Historical Thinking" by Fredrick D. Drake and Sarah Drake Brown fr an excellent instructional model for choosing and using different levels of primary sources.

Have an open mind, and think creatively. Be on the lookout for unconventional approaches to the content and interesting angles from which to present the subject. For example, rather than the social and political causes, the players, and battles, begin your study of the Civil War with a discussion of what average Americans currently do to support those in the armed forces. Follow with William Jones Rhees' 1902 article, "The Humanities of the War," what he calls the religious ministries, distribution of free reading material, commission to improve sanitary conditions, donations of personal necessities and writing materials, and aid to the wounded and dying. Rhees advances that the "Many volumes and thousands of pages of official reports, biographies, newspaper and magazine articles have recounted the work of those who aided the army by ministrations of love and charity and self-sacrificing devotion." These and others provided spiritual and physical comfort to the soldiers.

- The Sanitary Commission.
- The Christian Commission.
- The Young Men's Christian Association (publisher of the *Soldier's Pocket Companion.*
- Boston Tract Society (publisher of *The Knapsack Book*). (Rhees, 1902, pp. 165–66)

Start here, and just watch the questions your students ask. Their questions likely lead you to the issues, horrors, and complexities of the Civil War.

With a framework to work within, you have moved into document-based instruction, focused on primary sources that tell the story from the heart and mind of those who lived through the times. This puts you at a deeper level of insight where, through dynamic teaching, you model an excitement for stories as the puzzle pieces of history and show students how to apply what they discover to their understanding of humanity—themselves, others, and society.

Ideally, you are now a mini-expert with the excitement and confidence needed to teach the material well, just as you were when you wrote a research paper when you were in college. One of the perks of teaching is that you get to master an array of knowledge and skills in areas you might have once shunned or felt inept at. You can now teach with assurance and enjoyment, a testament to the old adage that the best way to learn something is to have to teach it.

It shouldn't be difficult to transfer this excitement to your students. Start advantageously by presenting something that piques their interest right away and neutralizes any thought of tuning-out. A good book, movie, or TV show hooks you from the start and compels you to stick with it, and so should your teaching. If the authors, directors, and actors lacked understanding and passion for their work or misread their audience, it would show in their product, just as it would show in your teaching.

Consider the driving passion in this poem about the first woman of mathematics, written as an alternative calculus project by a high school student who was good at math and loved stories and expressing herself through writing more.

> Hypatia of Alexandria
> By Jessica Manvell
>
> A man, Theon,
> obsessed with creating
> the perfect human being.
> A daughter, Hypatia,
> Born 370 A.D.
> Art, philosophy, literature, and science
> all taught to a little girl.
> A girl.
> Trained in speech, taught in Alexandria,
> sent to Athens to study.
>
> Traveling through Europe,
> gliding in and out of
> lives and minds,
> offering glimpses of beauty
> and tastes of brilliance.
> Proposed to by princes and philosophers,
> she had one answer:
> "I am already married to the truth."
> Thought and discovery were her life,
> not submissive silence
> in the presence of a man.
>
> She could not accept marriage
> or loyalty to a religion.

Questioning and analyzing interfered,
beliefs did not come easily
to this woman of such intellect.
Neoplatonism was her answer,
allowed her her questions,
her doubts,
allowed her an open mind.
In a time when religion was beginning its reign,
Hypatia believed only in possibilities.

Returning to her home,
she found marble fragments
and shards of ivory in ruins
at her feet.
The Christians' wild destruction
had left the University only
A shadow of its earlier days.
Still, Hypatia, was determined.
Geometry,
Astronomy,
and the new algebra
consumed her love and devotion.
When her students struggled,
she wrote commentary on Diophantus.
Then treatises,
and with her father, commentary on Euclid.
From Hypatia also came
a method to distill sea water,
an astrolabe to aid navigation,
a planisphere to chart the stars.

In Alexandria, Hypatia flourished;
her home an intellectual center,
her lectures well attended,
her mind a constant river of ideas.
Her students were in awe,
in love with her,
in love with her knowledge.
They exchanged ideas, called her a
genius,
an oracle,
the Muse.
For her beauty,
her intelligence,

> her contributions,
> and her spirit of learning,
> she was respected and revered.
>
> She was also hated.
>
> Cyril, Christian patriarch of Alexandria,
> was the enemy.
> Orestes and Cyrene,
> friends of Hypatia,
> begged her to stay out of danger.
>
> One day in 415
> a carriage was stopped on
> its way to the University.
> An angry mob dragged Hypatia out.
> She had become a pawn amidst
> anger and conflict of faiths.
>
> On that day, Hypatia fell.
> Her flesh was scraped by oyster shells,
> limbs torn from her strong and pure body,
> pieces thrown into a fire.
> Amidst the victorious chants
> of close-minded zealots,
> the first woman of mathematics
> disappeared
> into flames and smoke.
> (Manvell, 2001, pp.15–16)

Could something as simple as a poem be the hook, the catalyst that grabs and holds your students' attention? Teachers have a lot of competition in the attention-getting arena. There are so many distractions in play in students' lives with the plethora of recreational and entertainment choices available to them that are scary, in 3-D, sexually charged, violent, visually mesmerizing, fast paced, and geared to appeal to a base level of human nature. The content and your teaching approach do not need to mimic these influences; they do need to be interesting and relevant. Can you see how this poem, used well, has the elements of suspense and drama to rival a popular movie?

For students who are used to high-energy entertainment, you need:

- A positive learner-centered climate that makes them want to be in your classroom.

- Materials and learning activities chosen to meet their varied developmental needs.
- Content that is relevant to their lives.
- A hook to get things started.
- Motivating lessons that require active participation and personal accountability.

Just as exploring the humanities of the Civil War would be an atypical place to start a unit of study of the Civil War, so, too, would be any approach that avoids beginning a unit with a statement of topic, necessary vocabulary, and a timeline.

Free the students to tap into the depth of thought and insight that exists in each of them. Start by sharing a resource that is unexpected, without an introduction, in a way that makes them wrinkle their brows and ask questions. Let your primary resource introduce your topic and drive your instruction. Settle your students down and just start reading, telling a real-life story, or showing them artifacts. No introduction needed. Let them weave a story. Present scenarios and pose questions instead of merely disseminating information. Provide a meaty mystery, and set the detectives loose!

Be provocative. Create controversy, one of the most effective and neglected strategies in our classrooms. The National Council on Social Studies position statement about "Academic Freedom and the Social Studies Teacher" identifies controversy as a critical component of a viable teaching: "Controversial Issues [. . .] must be studied in the classroom without the assumption that they are settled in advance or that there is only one right answer in matters of dispute. The social studies teacher must approach such issues in a spirit of critical inquiry exposing the students to a variety of ideas, even if they are different from their own."

Get your students riled up about something related to academics for a change! The sponge strategy works well to start a unit of study or lesson. Before they enter the classroom, write a carefully selected, provocative quote on the board. They will notice it's there and read it, wondering why you wrote it. Ask them to discuss it with their peers. What does it mean? Why might you have chosen this particular quote? Bring them together to share and justify their ideas.

They are now hooked. Now keep up the interest. Parcel out relevant information and have them figure out the author's point of view in the context of what they now know. Let them identify things mentioned in the document that warrant further research. Ask them what they want to know more about. Guide them into making real world and personal connections with the material, and let them do something meaningful and real with what they have learned. Have them examine artifacts and make observations and predictions. Pass around the business card, political cartoon, newspaper article, quote, tool, and old photograph, and let students work with them to make meaning. When you get your students reacting to compelling materials and comfortable expressing their ideas, they are on the road to thinking like a historian.

A Socratic Seminar gives you and your students an empowering framework within which to respond to such primary materials. Give each student a copy of the same primary document (text, image, artwork, music) to thoroughly examine, and then lead them in a probing dialogue. In a Socratic Seminar, students, one at a time, respond to a question. They express their ideas, referring to the document to justify what they are saying. Questions stimulate thinking, and thinking triggers more questions that require deeper and deeper levels of reasoning.

This thoughtful, focused teaching process exposes students to different perspectives as they practice how to truly listen to and respect divergent ideas. The process is based on the premise that critical and creative thinking can be taught if students are posed open-ended questions and have a secure learning environment in which to respond. A Socratic Seminar using a primary source can serve as a stimulating introduction to a topic of study.

As with the Socratic Seminar, keep foremost in your mind who is doing most of the work during your lessons, who is actively thinking and talking. The answer should be the students—each one of them. Of course, you also work hard with much of your effort going to preparing beforehand and then to facilitating students' construction of knowledge and understanding during the lesson. Facilitating a Socratic Seminar is challenging. It takes practice and skill. Your hard work as the facilitator and questioner allows them the experience of a respectful exchange of ideas in a climate where they are expected to work hard. Their active involvement from start to finish is a product of inspired, comprehensive teaching that follows a natural learning cycle.

In *About Learning*, Bernice McCarthy proposes the "4-Mat Learning System," four quadrants of a circle that represent the natural, logical progression a learner makes from "personal meaning, to expert knowledge, to practical tinkering, and individual creativity" (McCarthy, 1996, p. 202). The cycle clarifies what we know about how people learn and applies beautifully to teaching history effectively.

Start by letting students find a reason to want to learn the concepts and material in the first place by getting and holding their attention. Next, give students the opportunity to learn the content and develop concepts and essential understandings by providing quality primary and secondary resources with which to work. Now it's time for students to apply and experiment with these concepts and knowledge through meaningful practical experiences. With the cycle nearing its end, challenge students to creatively extend their learning beyond what has been covered, to apply their conceptual and practical knowledge to new situations.

And smile with satisfaction as the cycle starts again.

My first elementary teaching position was in fourth grade in a rural school in upstate New York where the curriculum was based on the textbooks you found in the room. There was no district-defined scope and sequence to guide you, and it was before the advent of state and local standards, outcomes, and benchmarks. You were on your own, a far cry from the curricular parameters under which teachers now work.

What I found on the classroom shelf turned out to be as much a godsend as it was rare: It was a book of stories! The fourth-grade social studies textbook was a collection of biographies of notable people in American history. They were organized by category—inventors, adventurers, humanitarians, and leaders—who had each contributed to the fabric of our history. The stories were interesting and approachable, and they inspired further inspection of the circumstances and times surrounding their lives.

We were drawn in by the stories of these individuals. We identified their qualities, their contributions, and frailties, and researched their impact on society and place in history. Each biography led us to extension activities that cemented universal concepts and understandings along with a foundation of knowledge, and we had a good time doing it.

True, the individuals featured in the text were preselected and predigested by the publisher and not necessarily whom I might have chosen, yet at that point in time, I was happy to have a narrative-based, learner-centered way to teach history. I was free to include a more diverse group of Americans to study, which I did, and to go beyond the text with additional information and thought-provoking questions.

Most memorable for me was our humanitarian unit. After studying the lives of humanitarians and processing what they meant to us in our personal lives, we decided to try it ourselves. Each student made a functional work of art—vase, pencil holder, picture frame—and wrote a letter to a specific resident at the elderly care facility in a nearby village. With no money for buses, we established a time after school to meet there and asked parents to bring their child and a few other students if they could. These were country kids who lived up to ten miles from the village, so I knew I was asking a lot. I brought all their gifts in my car so I could personally deliver them for the students who couldn't make it.

You can probably see where I'm heading. The students were so intrinsically motivated and had such a depth of understanding and commitment to humanitarianism that nearly all twenty-five showed up! I was thrilled for all of them, and there was one boy who touched me in a special way.

He was a wiry, intelligent, sensitive child who did not always make the best behavior choices. I loved him. His parents were both profoundly deaf, and he was a hearing child who signed to communicate with them. His parents did not come in for conferences, and phone calls were not possible; we communicated through notes. Yet, there they both were at the senior center, sitting in their car, waiting with their son for me to arrive. My student must have told them that this was very important. He bounded out of the car with such enthusiasm I almost burst into tears, and I finally met his parents. He had a new sense of connection to school and to his own humanity, and he had shared it with his family.

The gifts the students presented were rustic, and the learning activity is not an extraordinary teaching idea by any means. Teachers are well-known for doing service projects more involved than this one, in and out of the school building. What is of particular note, though, is that it meant so much to my students that they mentioned it as their favorite activity of the year. The culmination of a social studies unit was their favorite learning experience, and their favorite new word of the year was integrity. I know this because in June, I asked them to evaluate our nine months together. Their comments made it clear to me that stories and personal connections were the underpinnings of a successful year teaching history and learning to be people of high character.

The project I just described resonated with my students on many levels. Most had elderly family members themselves—we lost a few grandparents that year. They were also at an age where they were increasingly aware of social issues and concerned with fairness. They loved a lively, thought-provoking discussion that applied this burgeoning awareness to current events. They were inspired to make a positive impact on the world. They learned what it meant to be a humanitarian, to help others out of a feeling of joint humanity, and I can only surmise they took this social construct with them into their adult lives.

Stories, such as these historical biographies, come alive with an audience and can be tailored for specific groups and ages. The presentation can be a simple gathering together for a story, as was traditionally done by Native Americans around the fire circle, and is now done by campers around a campfire. With a little ceremony and drama, such as low lighting, props, and a couple of unlit logs stacked in the middle of the students, the storytelling circle takes on a mystical quality. Black Elk of the Oglala Lakota Tribe, a participant in the 1876 Battle of Little Big Horn, Montana, explained this focus on circles: "You have noticed that everything an Indian does is in a circle and that is because the Power of the World always works in circles and everything tries to be round" (Black Elk, n.d.). What a beautiful concept and a wonderful basis for a conversation.

In an appealing atmosphere, the story has now been told. Thoughtful curiosity is piqued, establishing a bond with another time and place. It is time to ask students to relate to the individuals, comment on the choices made, ask questions about the circumstances, and to identify incongruities. This experience then springboards the class into a meaningful, engrossing study of history. You have addressed the content you need to cover, and through critical thinking, built concepts that are relevant enough to stick to the Velcro in the brain, available to be applied to the next story or personal experience. Your enthusiasm has successfully breathed life into history and inspired your students.

Be prepared. This is a powerful way to approach history. Once you and your students learn about the valiant and doomed Pickett's Charge on the third and final day of the vicious Battle of Gettysburg, from the view of both the North and of the South, and how thousands of proud Southern boys marched unwaveringly in battle formation across the long, exposed, grassy, treeless field toward the enemy, their company flags held high, all to the disbelief of the Union officers and soldiers watching from across the field behind the breastworks they had built for protection, with their artillery and

Photo 11.1 U.S. Army cannon facing the open field where Major General George Pickett and his men made their infamous July 3, 1863 charge, Gettysburg National Military Park. *Author's collection.*

muskets poised to stop what surely was a death march, and the unabashed regret and profound guilt of the South's beloved and trusted leader, General Robert E. Lee, who sent them out to their doom, and then hear about the record number of dead and wounded soldiers on both sides that lay slaughtered on that Pennsylvania battlefield that third day of July in 1863, you and your students will never again look at the world, war, courage, and the human condition in quite the same way.

This is the gift history offers us, one you can offer your students.

Chapter 12:

The Find: Historical Thinking at Work

"History is the record of encounters between character and circumstances."

—Donald Creighton

Serendipity. Many pivotal points in our lives are a case of serendipity. I could never have anticipated such a thing. Once we start experiencing history through primary sources, the story comes alive to us. Teachers need to have and share this passion for history. It can happen when you least expect it.

For me it was a typical morning. Buses were arriving, students were wandering into their respective classrooms. A sixth grader walked into our room with something in her hand to share. I looked at what she had and realized that this wasn't a typical "show-and-tell." Gripped in her hand was a pile of neatly folded, slightly faded letters that, she informed us, her family found in the attic of their barn.

She was holding a stack of handwritten letters from the 1860s! These were *original* Civil War era letters, from a Civil War soldier and his family, and she had brought them to school on the bus with no precautions to keep them safe. I immediately asked her if I could make copies of the letters, and it was a good thing I did. To this day, no one in the soldier's family knows where the originals are. They didn't even know they existed until I shared them.

The copies I made are the only known evidence of Van R. Strong's Civil War letters and his personal account of his experiences as a Union soldier.

One letter would have been enough to keep me interested for a while. A dozen and a half have occupied my time for decades. They elevated my passion for history to a new level of appreciation for the insight of those who lived during the times. This personal experience with raw primary documents led me to a compelling drive to know everything I could about a long-dead stranger. It

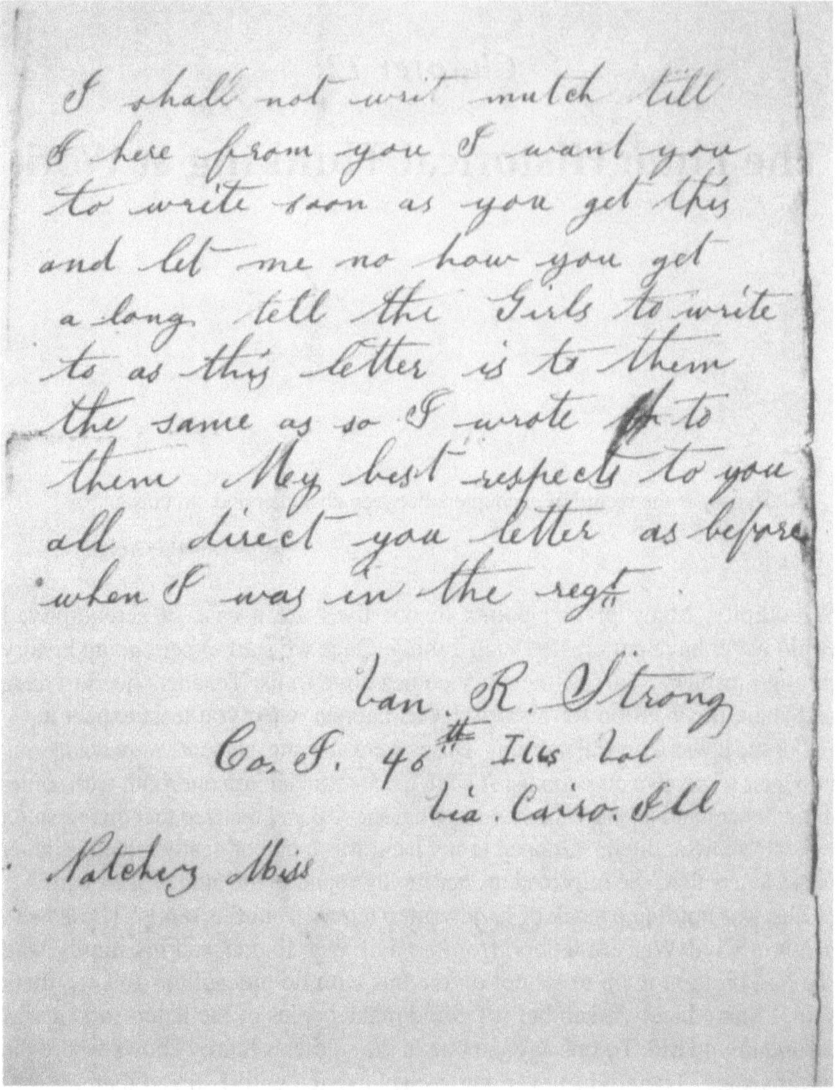

Photo 12.1 Closing lines of Van R. Strong's October 12, 1863, letter to his mother, Lydia Ann Strong. *Author's collection.*

was as if I physically stepped through the looking glass into the life of someone who lived before my parents and grandparents were even born. I now know him so well that he is a living presence in my life. I call him "my soldier."

As I pored over the handwritten letters, the lives of Van Rensselaer Strong and his family revealed themselves before my eyes. It was an intimacy not found in biographies and other secondary sources. It was akin to reading a journal, unpolished and from the heart, something private I should revere. It was the story of a soldier and the times he lived in, and it intrigued me. I was hooked.

I started out knowing absolutely nothing of the Strong family and was soon on a journey with them through mid-nineteenth century America. From the letters and my related research, I pieced together the core puzzle pieces—names, dates, places, property, and livelihoods—and slowly connected them with the personal story I uncovered. Later in my research, I had help from members of the Strong family who were surprised and thrilled to learn of the letters. I shared my photocopied versions of the letters with his descendants from three states—New York, Missouri, and Iowa—and we filled in gaps in the story for each other. My first glimpse of what Van looked like was from pictures the family sent me twenty years after I first read his name. This sharing relationship with Van's descendants continues today as I write this book. They are cheering me on.

The copies of the letters sat in a box for years before I decided to really study them. I had read them over many times, and now I intended to analyze them. My first task was to transcribe the letters, a job historians take seriously. Accuracy is paramount. The letters were written on both sides of thin paper, with a quill pen and black ink, in many cases with every inch of the surface of the paper crammed with writing (and some unintended blobs of ink), in the highly stylized cursive of the times, with permanent crease lines from folding. Punctuation and capitalization were rare, and spelling was often phonetic and creative. It took me quite a few rereadings and edits before I got them right. I had to learn new vocabulary. There are still a few words I cannot decipher.

Each letter presented pieces of the jigsaw puzzle while simultaneously triggering dozens more questions about Van, the mid-nineteenth century, and the war itself. The scope of the puzzle grew as a result. It evolved from an investigation of a man and his family to a study of a period in American history.

My search for answers followed a natural progression from the letters to Internet searches. Van, himself, provided me with a valuable advantage. He dated and signed each letter, and he identified his unit number and where he was when he wrote them. This was a tremendous help as I tried to figure out the progression of his army experience. I searched his name and his military regiment and struck gold when I discovered a site with a detailed history of each Illinois regiment and a list of those in that command. It was a turning point in my search.

I watched the Ken Burns' PBS documentary series, *The Civil War,* many times. It is built upon primary materials—photographs, diaries, news articles, speeches, and government and military communications. As I learned where Van and his brother and cousins were stationed and what battles they were

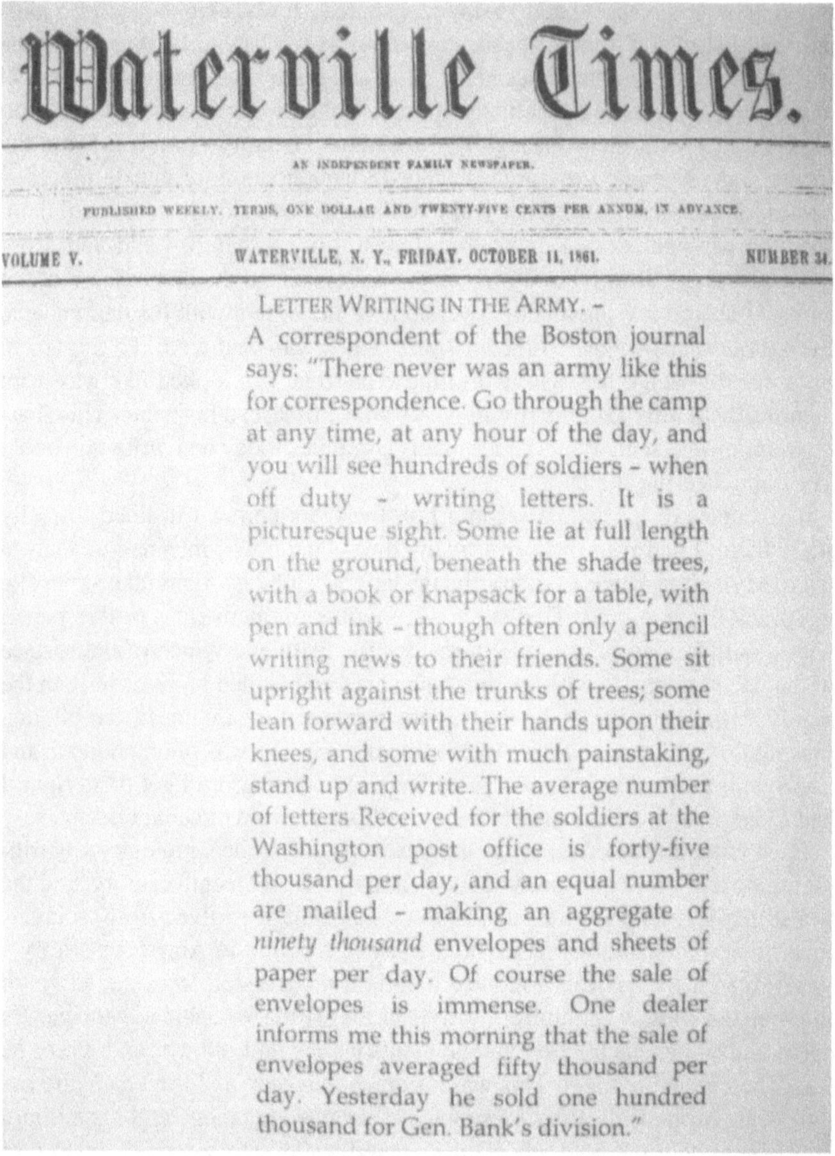

Waterville Times.

AN INDEPENDENT FAMILY NEWSPAPER.

PUBLISHED WEEKLY. TERMS, ONE DOLLAR AND TWENTY-FIVE CENTS PER ANNUM, IN ADVANCE.

| VOLUME V. | WATERVILLE, N. Y., FRIDAY, OCTOBER 11, 1861. | NUMBER 34. |

LETTER WRITING IN THE ARMY. – A correspondent of the Boston Journal says: "There never was an army like this for correspondence. Go through the camp at any time, at any hour of the day, and you will see hundreds of soldiers – when off duty – writing letters. It is a picturesque sight. Some lie at full length on the ground, beneath the shade trees, with a book or knapsack for a table, with pen and ink – though often only a pencil writing news to their friends. Some sit upright against the trunks of trees; some lean forward with their hands upon their knees, and some with much painstaking, stand up and write. The average number of letters Received for the soldiers at the Washington post office is forty-five thousand per day, and an equal number are mailed – making an aggregate of *ninety thousand* envelopes and sheets of paper per day. Of course the sale of envelopes is immense. One dealer informs me this morning that the sale of envelopes averaged fifty thousand per day. Yesterday he sold one hundred thousand for Gen. Bank's division."

Photo 12.2 October 11, 1861, newspaper article, "Letter Writing in the Army," from the *Waterville Times. Courtesy of the Waterville Times, Waterville, New York.*

engaged in, I went back to the series to review those particular events, this time with firsthand insight and an eye on details.

Other primary sources provided background information and corroborated specifics mentioned in the letters. Using information on the Internet, including government records, letters written by other Civil War soldiers (including two from his regiment), original military field records, old maps, and county and town records, one site led to another, and the pieces started to fit in. Each piece, no matter how small, was something to celebrate. I called it my goose chase, and it was thrilling. I found I couldn't stop until I uncovered the full story, from birth to death. I wanted to connect the dots but only with legitimate sources.

Studying these primary documents, which soon included the property deeds of the Sellecks who lived next to the Strong family in New York, Van's individual military records, newspaper obituaries and their accompanying testimonials, and rereading the letters dozens of times and looking up vocabulary I was unfamiliar with was an experience of repeated "ah-has" and clues to explore:

- Oh, that's what that word is!
- This name sounds familiar—aren't they buried in the same cemetery?
- That date can't be correct because the census says he was still living in New York.
- Yes, his regiment was at the Battle of Pittsburg Landing on the dates he mentions, and it was raining that day, just like he describes!

The discoveries gave me a rush of adrenaline and fueled my need to learn more. I wasn't studying the Civil War per se. I was trying to understand Van's life. The two had become so intertwined I couldn't help but learn an amazing amount about the war and those tumultuous times. I'm not alone in my fascination with the Civil War. Far from it. It is a wildly popular topic, and many have made it their life's hobby. Every year, there are dozens of Civil War encampments and reenactments around the country that preserve the history and provide authentic living history experiences. I recently attended one as part of my research.

Why this fascination? The Civil War is our war and ours alone. It is glamorized with tales of heroes and villains on both sides. It happened on U.S. soil, right where we live today, and there are battlefields and historic markers to remind us of what happened and where. All the casualties were American, and the ramifications of the conflict affected everyone. The American people were polarized and, as with a family fight, it was personal. We were fighting ourselves and not with words anymore; now it was with cannons and muskets, and it was for keeps.

The legacy of slavery still affects and haunts us. It is potent. Many Americans have ancestors who fought and died in the war or who were slaves finally freed by the Emancipation Proclamation. For some, the history passed down through the generations still festers with anger about slavery and the shame of losing the war.

Learning about the antebellum South and the war years gives us a window into our developing nation and the diversity of thought and traditions of our people, especially the competing needs of the North and South. It isn't difficult to do this. Information is easily accessed by visiting historic sites, through examining written records, diaries, letters, and photographs, and, for some, by looking at their own family history. Primary documents help us cut through the spin and revisionist history and ground us to what really did happen. We are free to explore the meaning, to go past the lore to the plausible truth, and apply lessons learned.

When the governor of Virginia declared April 2010 to be Confederate History Month, the issues were once again front-page. Not only was the state seen as glorifying what is still an emotionally charged piece of American history, a war that was fought to form a separate country to protect the institution of slavery, the proclamation failed to even mention slavery.

Ken Burns, producer of the acclaimed PBS series I mentioned, who is accepted as a leading authority on the Civil War, responded in Devon Dwyer's April 28, 2010, ABC News interview entitled "More Traumatic than 9/11? A Fresh Look at the Civil War 150 Years Later," "As long as we exclude huge portions of our past and use the past to serve as a political vehicle now, we do a disservice to everyone," said Burns. "The Civil War involved four million human beings that were owned by other human beings in a country that had declared to the world all men are created equal. That's why the Civil War happened" (Dwyer, Devin, 2010, p.2).

Four million.

The Civil War is not over. Racism and its fallout is still a palpable undercurrent of American society. The delineation between Federal and State's rights is still a hot issue, as witnessed by the rise of the Tea Party organization. Some reactionary patriot groups want to form their own militias to protect their states from the U.S. government. Still, it is almost unfathomable that in the twenty-first century, one state, let alone eleven, would secede from the United States of America and form a separate country.

Yet, that was what happened in 1861, just as Lincoln was assuming the presidency of this polarized country. The Southern states and the Northern states had profound fundamental differences, serious enough for South

Carolina, North Carolina, Florida, Tennessee, Georgia, Alabama, Mississippi, Virginia, Louisiana, Arkansas, and Texas to take such a bold and treasonous step as to form the Confederate States of America.

Lincoln faced this crisis frankly in his March 4, 1861, inaugural address. His closing remarks appeal to our joint position as American citizens and his duty to protect that union:

> You have no oath registered in heaven to destroy the Government, while I shall have the most solemn one to "preserve, protect, and defend it."
> I am loath to close. We are not enemies, but friends. We must not be enemies. Though passion may have strained, it must not break our bonds of affection. The mystic chords of memory, stretching from every battlefield and patriot grave to every living heart and hearthstone all over this broad land, will yet swell the chorus of the Union, when again touched, as surely they will be, by the better angels of our nature.

At the suggestion of his Secretary of State, William Seward, this last paragraph of Lincoln's first inaugural address replaced his original final words, "Shall it be peace or sword?" Seward, Lincoln's rival for the 1860 Republican presidential nomination, and later a most loyal member of his cabinet, thought it prudent to strike a more hopeful tone. It didn't help (Lincoln, 1861, March 4).

The 1859 essay by Dresser proposed thinly-veiled justifications to continue the practice of slavery expressed in beliefs that the rights of individuals, interpretation of the seventy-year-young U.S. Constitution, and separation of the powers of the State and the Federal governments were at the heart of the conflict. Others would say straightforwardly that the brewing conflict was from the growing clamor for the civil rights of slaves and women and the evils of and limitations on the expansion of slavery. These antislavery arguments threatened destruction of the over two hundred year history of the institution of slavery itself.

My childhood trips to Civil War sites, along with my fascination with Abraham Lincoln and lifelong commitment to civil rights and racial equality, had already established my intrinsic interest. As it turned out, the letters fell into good hands. The letters brought me to an entirely different level of personal connection. I have a working-level understanding of American and world history, but when it comes to the Civil War, I am now quite well-versed—a mini-expert—and inspired to share what I know with anyone who cares to listen. The stories and universal concepts and essential understandings are as relevant today as they were in 1860 and serve as proof that we can and should learn from history.

I shake my head in disbelief when I picture what these soldiers and the country went through.

Chapter 13:

Eking Out the Story

"Knowledge of history frees us to be contemporary."

—Lynn Write, Jr.

These primary sources, found in a farmhouse barn in rural Madison County, upstate New York, provided a wealth of details, inferences, vocabulary, colloquialisms, nuances, and off-handed remarks from which to work. The journey to knowing and understanding was a process of constantly asking questions, finding clues, gathering information, recognizing the significance of small details, enjoying the unexpected, and forming concepts into the big picture. It took tenacity, a great deal of historical thinking, and a healthy dose of intuition.

There are ample archived record repositories to more than feed a historian's curiosity. Military records are accessible on the Internet at the National Park Service's *Civil War Soldiers and Sailors System,* by request at the National Archives and Records Administration, and at individual state websites. In my journey, I examined Van Strong's military and pension records, given to me by one of his descendents who had already requested them from the federal government.

In addition, at the Cornell *Making of America* site, those invaluable accounts of the day-to-day activities of the war, I read the original army field officer's reports that pertained to events mentioned in the letters. I was able to compare Van's version of events with the official reports, and, from what I've uncovered, he gave an accurate account of his regiment's participation in the war. The records and his letters corroborate each other.

It is interesting that there was no censorship of the thousands upon thousands of letters Civil War soldiers sent home. If the letters were intercepted, they could easily have provided the enemy with information to use against them. This was not the way the government approached World War II eighty years later, when the U.S. Armed Forces made sure military personnel knew in no uncertain terms that "loose lips sink ships." Letters were read and censored before they were sent on to the recipient, casual talk about military subjects and boasting were prohibited, and, if captured by the enemy, it was name, grade, and serial number, nothing more. World War II mail going to or from the military was read and put on microfilm and printed on what they called V Mail. There was tight government control and no expectation of privacy.

For background, I read non-fiction books about the Civil War and Abraham Lincoln and historical fiction stories set in mid-nineteenth century America. I read the pertinent regimental histories, Grand Army of the Republic memoirs and reunion materials, and scoured government, family, and local historical records, and genealogy websites, all the while building a greater understanding of the times, constantly finding something new to research. The more I learned, the better a researcher I became. I had something to which I could attach new bits of information and a stream of new leads. I would do research for hours and lose track of time.

As I verified the accuracy of dates, names, and places Van and his brother and cousins mentioned, I developed an understanding of the context in which the letters were written. I leaned a new vocabulary of the times and I pinpointed on maps the places I came across in my search, calculated distances, and traced routes. I read letters from many Civil War soldiers in other regiments, North and South, offering varying points of view and further insight into the soldiers' experiences and the importance of letter-writing. In the letters, I saw differences in perspectives, concerns, and educational levels of the writers. This again drove home the influence exerted by individual perspective and bias. Whatever I read, I was sure to consider the source with the obvious factors of North or South and the point of time in the war when it was written.

Researching a real person gave me a better understanding of the history of the period than basic facts and battle summaries did. I started to feel what it was like to live back then. I came to realize how complicated and devastating the period was for all Americans and how the Federal government held the Union together thanks to superior numbers of fighting men and a thin, frayed thread of lucky breaks. In no stretch of the imagination was it glamorous.

These primary and secondary sources were augmented by field research. I was curious to see what the specific area where Van grew up looked like and if I could use my wits to locate them in person. I had that luxury since I lived only an hour from Perryville in Madison County, New York, Van's family homestead. Perryville was not far from the school where I had taught, and the whole letter adventure began. The barn where the letters were found could have been one on the Selleck farm, not far away.

One summer, I dedicated my available time to getting away from the computer and into the places where this history happened. I drove the back roads of beautiful, rural Madison County, much of which had changed little since Van was around. I brought my research materials with me to refer to as I hiked the fields, looked for hidden family cemeteries, visited area libraries, and spoke with local historians.

Throughout this quest, I came across helpful people who enthusiastically shared what they knew with me. They were people also intrigued by good stories and the sense of history inherent in every spot on earth. I continue to benefit from the collections and information of people I come in contact with, including Deb Moses, who, when I told her what my book was about, graciously loaned me four years worth of original Civil War letters written by two of her Illinois ancestors, along with memorabilia that had been passed down through generations. Coincidentally, the brothers were from the same Illinois county as Van.

There is no better example of this spirit than when I stopped at the house where Van's neighbors, the Selleck family, once lived. Van regularly made fond references to them in his letters home. The location of the property was just as the huge, old map on the Morrisville College library wall indicated.

The current owner of the Selleck property listened to my story and looked at my documents. He promptly showed me around the farm and pointed out where the Strong family likely lived—in the small, clapboard cape cod a short way from the big house. He and his wife invited me inside their beautiful old farmhouse and brought out all the deeds and other records they had for the property. The documents went back to the early 1800s, when Drake Selleck bought the first acreage. Over a glass of lemonade, we looked at the papers, matching names and dates, sharing what we each knew.

He then did a remarkable thing: he gave me the original property documents to take with me to copy and return to him when I was done. Talk about trust! It tells you something about the nature of the people of rural upstate New York and the way a love of history can bring people together. We shared a mutual respect and appreciation for historical records. I copied the deeds and abstracts and returned them as soon as possible. I didn't want him to have one moment of doubt about his decision to trust me with his treasure.

Another unexpected turn of events during my research was an e-mail experience. In close proximity and unbeknownst to each other, I received e-mail inquires from two of Van R. Strong's descendants. While researching their ancestors, they had come across the transcriptions of Van's letters

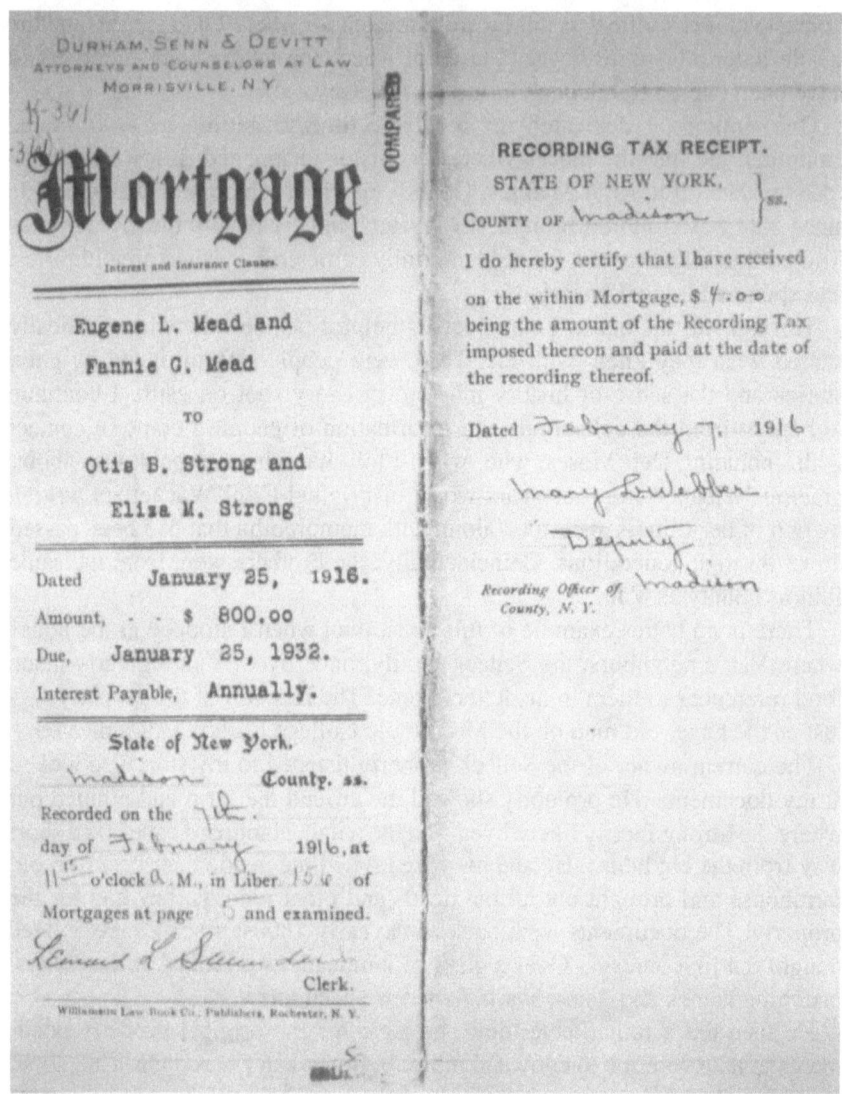

Photo 13.1 January 25, 1916, property deed for sale of 54 acres of Selleck farmland by Mary Strong Mead's son, Eugene, to Otis Strong. Ingalls Corners Road, Perryville, New York. *Author's collection.*

I had posted on the Illinois genealogy website, www.illgenweb.com, some years before. They were as surprised about the existence of the letters as I was to hear from them. My first Strong family contact was Van's great-grandson, Bob Campain. We exchanged information, and I soon became acquainted with Van's great-granddaughter, Arlene Showers, her husband

Don, their son and his wife, David and Lisa, and granddaughter, Becky. Bob and Arlene were not previously acquainted and were excited to find out they were both direct descendants of Van R. Strong and first cousins a few times removed.

The group of us wrote excited e-mails and began sharing our respective puzzle pieces. Bob gave us copies of Van's military records and his request for a disability pension, along with a photograph of Van's Iowa gravesite. Arlene's family, who were already avid genealogists, gave us family photographs and stories and names and details in the Strong lineage to check out.

Bob donated a copy of the massive two-volume set of Benjamin Dwight's *History of the Strong Family, The History of the Descendants of Elder John Strong of Northampton Massachusetts*, originally printed in 1871, along with volumes of updates from 1871–1990 to the Morrisville College Library. It was the Morrisville College librarian's local history website that got me started in my field research and whose huge wall map from 1859 first showed me exactly where the Selleck and Strong families had lived. There have been so many wonderful connections such as these.

One thing led to another, and in the year following my summer of field research, Arlene and her family—three generations of Strong descendants—came from Missouri to New York for a grand tour of the countryside where their ancestors once lived. I introduced them to the Strong family homes and gravesites I had located. We had the best time driving around, taking pictures, visiting cemeteries, seeing the Erie Canal, and putting together more pieces of Van R.'s story. Thanks to the Showers family, I had pictures and family lore to put with the names, and even more exciting, I had met some of his flesh and blood.

Our connection didn't end there. Several years later, we all met in Plainfield, Illinois, Van's adopted home on the "western frontier." A local self-made historian, Caron Stillmunkes, was researching every name on the Plainfield Soldiers' Memorial for a book of biographies she was writing. She was putting together a book of stories, and Van was one of them!

When looking for information about Van, Caron came across those same letters I had posted on the Illinois Genealogy Web site. She then contacted the Showers family and me. We again eagerly shared information with her and agreed to all meet at the monument in the spring, when the Illinois weather was more hospitable. In April, I flew to Plainfield from California, and the Showers family drove up from Missouri.

Caron had already contacted a reporter from the local Plainfield newspaper, *The Enterprise*. She thought readers would be interested in the story of how this random group of unrelated people, who lived in three different states, had found each other. Shannon McCarthy, the Enterprise reporter, listened well that drizzly morning while we sometimes talked over each other in

Photo 13.2 An artifact—the locket Van R. Strong carried with him while a Union soldier in the 46th Illinois Volunteer Infantry, now with his and his daughter and granddaughter's photograph. *Author's collection.*

excitement, and then wrote an eloquent, accurate, detailed newspaper article and doing so created a primary source—a record of our meeting.

At lunch, as we celebrated Arlene's eighty-sixth birthday in her great-grandfather's adopted hometown of Plainfield, I had the privilege of holding something that belonged to Van: an artifact, something very dear to him. It was the gold locket he carried with him during the war. I had made the journey from a pile of random letters to a wealth of information, insight, and a new family.

Caron's quest took another interesting twist when, while researching Captain Edward McAllister, one of the names on the Soldiers' Monument, she discovered his great-granddaughter had his original Civil War letters. I soon had the transcript of a letter where Captain McAllister mentioned my soldier by name! It turned out that Van and Captain McAllister knew each other before they both enlisted from Plainfield in 1861. McAllister's letter gave me a firsthand perspective of the kind of person Van was from a contemporary who knew him well. The story kept coming together.

Chapter 14:

Compelled to Share

"When a writer talks about his work, he's talking about a love affair."

—Alfred Kazin

With my teacher's sensibilities and my love of history and making connections, I knew I had to share the story of my quest and what I had learned. It was, and still is, a profound, personal experience. While I didn't know what form this sharing would take, I felt it could inspire teachers to use the stories waiting to be discovered in primary documents and artifacts.

What follows next is a biographical account of the Strong family of Perryville, New York, and Plainfield, Illinois. I created this reliable secondary source using all I learned about Van and his family from their letters, family, and official records, supplemented with the background information about the times and places. Especially helpful was chapter 6 of the *1880 History of Chenango and Madison Counties*, found at www.rootsweb.com.

Once you have this family background and read his sister Lydia's letter, the story picks up in August 1861, at the beginning of the Civil War, with Van's first letter to his mother. Included are verbatim, undoctored transcripts of the letters and a photocopy of the first letter in Van's own handwriting. The original provides authenticity and the immediacy inherent in primary documents, and they show you with what I had to work.

Van's letters span the years 1861 to 1865 and were written to his mother, Lydia Ann, his sister, Mary, and his younger brother, Otis. Van tells his story through these pure and simple communications written to his family. Also included are a few revealing letters from his siblings and from two of his Mitchell cousins, who had also lived in Madison County, New York, before they emigrated to Illinois, and then further west.

The Enterprise, Thursday, May 14, 2009 .... Page 3

Following his footsteps: Civil War letters lead soldiers' descendants to Plainfield, bring history buffs together

By Shannon McCarthy

A stack of old letters — forgotten in a barn for decades — brought three strangers together in Plainfield a few weekends ago.

They all came to Settlers' Park to view the Soldiers' Monument, etched with the name of the man responsible for linking the three women, who share a love of history and a penchant for genealogy.

Now, they also share a connection to Van R. Strong, a Civil War soldier from New York who enlisted from Plainfield 148 years ago.

The story got its start more than 20 years ago, when a student walked into Liz Manvell's classroom in Madison County, New York, clutching a bundle of letters.

"A student came to school with a handful of Civil War letters," she said.

"Seeing the original, handwritten letters, Manvell said, "I was beside myself."

After making photocopies of all the letters, Manvell began to read them carefully, studying the correspondence between Van Strong and his mother and sisters.

Manvell posted the letters online at ilgenweb.net, a site frequented by history buffs.

She also became curious about the Strong family and began tracing their lineage.

But she wasn't the only one. In Missouri, Lisa Showers was also researching the Strong family tree.

Her husband, Dave, is Van Strong's great-great grandson. Arlene Showers, Dave's mother, said she grew up hearing stories about her great-grandfather, who settled in Iowa and raised a family after the war.

"I heard a lot about old Van," said Arlene, who grew up in Iowa near the Strong family homestead.

"Grandma talked about him a lot."

Arlene, who lived with her grandmother for a time, also grew up fascinated with reminders of Van Strong's wartime service.

"My grandmother's sister Phoebe lived across the garden," she said.

"She had his uniform, his gun and a box of mementos."

While these artifacts have been lost, Arlene has reminders of her connection to the Strong family

The name of Van Strong's wife, Martha Hodge, has been kept alive over the generations.

"My mother is Martha," said Arlene, who also named her daughter after the family matriarch.

Today, a locket that once belonged to Van Strong is owned by another Martha — Arlene's great-granddaughter.

Van carried the locket, containing a lock of his beloved Martha's hair, while he fought in the Civil War.

See History buffs - next page

PHOTO BY SHANNON MCCARTHY
From left, Liz Manvell, Lisa Showers, Dave Showers, Arlene Showers and Don Showers pose in front of the Soldiers' Monument in Settlers' Park. Manvell connected with the Showers family after discovering a series of letters written by Showers family patriarch Van R. Strong during the Civil War.

Photo 14.1 Newspaper article from the Plainfield, Illinois, *Enterprise* telling the story of the April 2009 meeting of the Van R. Strong enthusiasts. *Courtesy of the Plainfield Enterprise, Plainfield, Illinois.*

The experience of researching the story of the letters moved me to an unexpected depth of understanding of the complexities and peculiarities of the Civil War and those who lived through it. The more I learned, the more questions I had; I'm still discovering things to research and filling in gaps in my knowledge. My accounts of the war are by no means exhaustive and should be recognized as such.

The letters are connected by a historically accurate Civil War story based on Van's life. Important to note is that other than what I learned from the letters and military records, there is no way to know exactly what Van said, thought, and did during this time. Therefore, the resulting piece, *From Farmer to Fighter,* is historical fiction, supported by primary and secondary sources. I strive to tell a story faithful to what he revealed of himself in his letters, fleshed out by my research, what his family told me of him, and the history of America during the Civil War.

Van's is the story of America in the mid-nineteenth century. It touches on all aspects of life as it explores the history of United States law, attitudes toward human rights, economics, medicine, family life, politics, government, religion, art, philosophy, the military, transportation, and technology. My investigation prompted me to ask and answer many questions, such as these that follow. Reading just one of the letters could be the hook that gets students' attention and prompts them to want to know the whole story.

- How did migration west contribute to the rising conflict between North and South?
- What were the politicians/governments (North and South) fighting for?
- What did the soldiers (North and South) believe they were fighting for?
- What role did Lincoln play before and during the War of the Rebellion?
- What did the slaves think the war was about, and how were they treated before and after emancipation and as soldiers in the Union Army?
- Why did so many soldiers die or get wounded in each battle, to eventually total more casualties than all the previous American wars combined?
- Why would a soldier reenlist to stay in the army if he had the chance to go home?
- What made soldiers go AWOL or desert for good, and how were they treated if caught?
- What happened if the enemy captured a soldier?
- How were families affected? Was it different in the North and the South?
- How were soldiers, North and South, treated by their governments (pay, food rations, clothing, supplies, discipline)?
- What did they do with their time when they weren't in a battle, on a march, or sick in the camp hospital?
- How did the quality of the military leaders on each side affect the outcome of the war?
- How might a soldier's view of war change over time?

I can only imagine Van never thought that a stranger might someday read and be fascinated by his letters, and surely not 150 years later. It is possible he didn't even know his family had saved them. Nor would he think his words would help us research and better understand the times. Van and the family member that tucked away the letters in the attic of that barn in Madison County left us quite a gift.

Chapter 15:

Meet the Strong Family

Crowded. Ten people in a small house: seven siblings, a mother and father, and a paternal grandfather made a crowd. Van Rensselaer Strong's family was an average-sized household for the times. It was the 1840s, and these ten people were trying to make a life for themselves.

Grandfather Lemuel Strong was born in Massachusetts ten years before the Revolutionary War, a war in which his father, Lt. Noah Strong, fought. With his young wife and second-born son dead, Lemeul pulled up his New England roots and took young Lewis to the open frontier of upstate New York.

At twenty-seven, Lewis met and married Lydia Ann Bugbee and soon started a family. They had three sons: Nelson Philester (also called Philester, Lester, Lest) and Vanrensselaer (Van, Van R., Vance) who were just a year apart in age, and Otis (Oat), younger by some fifteen years.

Sandwiched between Philester, the oldest child, and Otis, the youngest of all the children, were the three sisters Lydia Ann, Ada (Adah) Philura, and Mary (Moly) Bigelow. There was Lydia Ann, the mother, and Lydia Ann, the daughter. It was not unusual to give a son or daughter the same name as the parent or sibling and to see the same names repeated generation after generation. There was a fourth sister, Lucinda, who died when she was just ten. This was also common for the times. Cemeteries from the nineteenth century are lined with headstones and tiny markers for infants and children who died early in their lives and for mothers who died young, often in childbirth and from illness. We were many years away from understanding germs and sanitation and practical treatment of infections.

Philester, Van, and Otis were country boys, raised with their hands dirty and mud and snow on their shoes. The Strong house was located in the Lenox and Fenner part of Madison County, right in the geographical center of New

York State. This was lake-effect snow country where Lake Ontario plays a big part in the multiple feet of snowfall the area receives each year.

Madison County was far from bustling New York City, which was 275 miles to the southeast, both by distance and culture. The two areas could not have been more different and still been part of the same state. Rural Madison County sat halfway between the state capital city of Albany on the Hudson River to the east and the city of Buffalo on Lake Erie to the west, and was traversed by the Erie Canal completed in 1820.

This was the land of the Iroquois, the Haudenosaunee people, who ruled themselves by democratic principles. The land had been fought over many times since the Europeans moved in, with the Iroquois being the ultimate losers. Their land was taken outright or traded away for next-to-nothing, and then developed by the new American settlers sweeping west from New England. These settlers believed that if you paid for land or if the government made a treaty to get hold of it, you owned it outright.

The Cayuga, Mohawk, Oneida, Onondaga, Seneca, and Tuscarora tribes of the Iroquois League believed differently. In their Iroquois culture, the land was not theirs to own, but theirs to use with respectful care. The people of the longhouse were farmers and hunters and saw themselves as stewards of their natural surroundings.

The Iroquois knew very well that central New York was rich land with an abundance of trees, lakes, rivers, streams, and wild animals to hunt. They had lived off the land for a thousand years. Europeans, seeing themselves as the more civilized people and aided by the annihilation of native peoples by European diseases, claimed and seized it as their own and encouraged others to move and settle there. They eventually pushed out the Iroquois, forcing them to move further west, leaving their abundant woodlands and their way of life behind.

Many of the farms settled by Europeans in the tiny hamlet of Perryville in Madison County were a modest, productive succession of semi-rectangular plats laid out and sold to adventurous settlers. The Strong home was in what they called the Lenox Mile Strip and had a view that took your breath away.

Standing on the farm along Cranson Ridge, at 1200 feet above sea level, you could see the fertile valley below, stretching for ten miles north all the way to sprawling Oneida Lake. It was a large lake, reaching as far away as Syracuse, some twenty-one miles to the west. It was easy to imagine the barges of the Erie Canal, pulled by mules trudging along the canal towpaths, that entered into the lake on one end and emerged again at the other end, continuing on their way west to Buffalo and beyond, or back east to Albany and the Atlantic Ocean. Thomas Allen's 1905 song about the Erie Canal, "Low Bridge, Everybody Down," is a favorite folksong about this amazing technological feat (Thomas Allen, 1905, as cited in Erie Canal Village).

Thomas S. Woodcock's 1836 journal paints a firsthand picture of the canal system and explains why everybody had to get down:

> The Bridges on the Canal are very low, particularly the old ones. Indeed they are so low as to scarcely allow the baggage to clear, and in some cases actually rubbing against it. Every Bridge makes us bend double if seated on anything, and in many cases you have to lie on your back. The Man at the helm gives the word to the passengers: "Bridge," "very low Bridge," "the lowest in the Canal," as the case may be. Some serious accidents have happened for want of caution. (Woodcock, 1836 as cited in *Eye Witness to History*)

The energizing effect of the Erie Canal on the local economy waned as the railroads expanded and outpaced the canals in expedience. According to the gazetteers of the times, which are geographic reference books of descriptive or statistical information such as dictionaries or indexes of places (www.encarta.msn.com), the population of central New York actually decreased from the mid-to-late nineteenth century. Thanks to Daniel H. Weiskottenn's compilation, "Descriptions of Town of Fenner, Madison County, NY, in 19th Century Gazetteers," we get a good sense of how the Town of Fenner and Perryville were fairing.

The gazetteers tell us Fenner, of which the hamlet of Perryville was the main population center, was not a boom area by any means. It had a population of 1,972 in 1835, 1,997 in 1840, and then dropped to 1,690 in 1850 (the time when Van, his sisters, Mitchell relatives, and other neighbors started their emigration to the Midwest). In 1860, there were 1,649 residents, and at the end of the Civil War in 1865, the population was 1,387. By 1892, the number of residents of the town of Fenner had fallen to a mere 999.

According to John Disternell's 1843 description of Perryville itself, the hamlet had 250 residents, forty dwelling houses, one church, one tavern, one store, one flouring mill, one tannery, and one distillery. In 1873, Franklin Hough's Gazetteer of the State of New York said Perryville consisted of two churches, a gristmill, a sawmill, and thirty-five houses, (as cited in Weiskottenn, 1999), showing a loss of five dwellings and the tavern, tannery, distillery, and store.

The Strongs did not own the small house where the family lived or the land where they grew sweet corn, pumpkins, tobacco, and apples and kept chickens for eggs. Mr. Drake Selleck and his son, William, in the big farmhouse next door, owned it. The Sellecks and a few other families owned most of the land from Perryville Road up Ingalls Corners Road along that stretch of the mile strip. The land offered good grazing for livestock. Next to the Selleckes' property were the Van Epps and Van Duesen farms, family-owned and worked by laborers like the Strongs. Many of the settlers of Perryville had

Photo 15.1 Plainfield Settlers' Monument, part of an informative marker and timeline project at the Plainfield Settlers' Park. *Author's collection.*

first come to New York from Massachusetts and Connecticut, and England, Scotland, and Holland before that. The Van Epps and Van Duesens remind us of the Dutch immigrants who settled in New York State and that New York City was once called New Amsterdam.

Lewis, Philester, and Van were farm laborers, hired hands. It was common to live on a piece of land and work it for someone else, that is, until you made enough money to buy your own, or you were willing to pick up and head west where the land was cheap and plentiful, and even free to homesteaders.

The land was parceled into tracts and sold off to settle and stabilize the still-unpopulated land farther west and to further push the Native Americans out of the way. There was no question about who would triumph. The indigenous people had little power against the well-armed, disease-carrying Europeans. The adventurous pioneers considered the continent to be wide-open space, waiting to be settled. Under the policy of manifest destiny and the Preemption Act of 1841 and the Homestead Acts of 1832 and 1862, the U.S. government helped claim it for the United States of America. The goal was to keep it from being claimed by other countries and to add to the number of states in the union (Homestead Acts, www.ourdocuments.gov).

By the 1850s, Central New York, well-populated and still rural with small towns and hamlets, was no longer called the wild frontier. With the rest of the North American continent opening up, the line of the western frontier had moved further west, and in the pioneer spirit of adventure and possibilities, many folks were drawn to follow.

Far out west along the coast of the Pacific Ocean was an exotic, promising place called California. Native Americans, Mexican Californios, and Spanish missionaries populated the sprawling region. In 1848, gold was discovered at Sutter's Mill on the South Fork of the American River, and a flood of dreamers came looking for riches. The region soon teemed with people from all over the world. It was a treacherous journey to get there, by land or sea, and not all who set out for California made it. When they did, there were escalating animosities among the Native Americans, who already inhabited the land, and among the different nationalities, and a ruthless conflict to contend with as they competed for the dwindling placer gold and sparse mother lodes. Once they came, they stayed, and California became the thirty-first state in 1850.

Van was nearing twenty in 1850, a natural age for a son to strike out on his own, and the decade was a boom time for the north central states. Van wasn't interested in moving farther west to look for gold as was his Mitchell cousin John. He wanted to farm good land. Midwest production of dairy products and crops had grown dramatically over the past decade, and Illinois, Iowa, and Wisconsin promised a rich life for all who ventured there. He likely heard about this area from his Mitchell relations and the many Perryville neighbor folks who had already moved there.

By 1850, Van shows up on the Wisconsin Census. He had traveled from the rolling hills, deciduous and coniferous forests, and bubbling creeks and waterfalls of Madison County across Pennsylvania, Ohio, Indiana, and Illinois, and north to Wisconsin, part of the sprawling prairie land of the Great Plains. He was blessed to not have to cross the troublesome Rockies. Some of those gold-seeking "forty-niners" and emigrant families did not survive the journey through the treacherous mountain passes and Indian country.

When Van arrived in Wisconsin, he found a grassy, flat terrain, kept treeless by frequent brush fires, and easy to farm ("What is a Prairie?" n.d.). It was different from upstate New York. The steep hills and uneven terrain of Mr. Selleck's land meant backbreaking work getting the soil free of rocks, the land cleared of trees, ready to plant, and then caring for it once the crops were in. The miles of stonewalls winding up and down and around the hillsides of New York State serving as property lines and fences around homes and cemeteries were testament to the physical labor required to farm. Here on the prairie, in place of stonewalls, you could picture rows and rows of corn.

Everyone knew about the never-ending pounding wind and blasting snow on the prairie. One thing the two areas did share was the changeable weather, summer humidity, and lake-effect snow and winds. This unpredictable weather of the plains was of little concern to someone from upstate New York. Van was used to long, cold, and snowy winters, late, muddy springs, and hot and humid summers. Perryville had taught him how to plant what you can, when you can, where you can, and to survive the frigid months when nothing grew.

This prairie land at Koshkonong, Wisconsin, was fertile, and as the word spread that there was money to be made and adventures to be had in the Midwest, towns sprouted up everywhere, especially along rivers, canals, near train stations, and on stagecoach routes. A few years had passed as Van worked the land and fell into being a westerner when two of his sisters moved to Will County, Illinois. Lydia and Ada had caught the pioneer spirit and were now having an adventure of their own in the nearby bustling city of Joliet.

Joliet had experienced a recent growth spurt of its own due to the Chicago & Rock Island Railroad and the Illinois and Michigan Canal that ran through the city. The first train cruised the tracks from Chicago to Joliet on October 10, 1852 (rockrail.com), and two years before that, the I&M Canal began operations, connecting the Erie Canal—and thus the Atlantic Ocean—to the Mississippi River, which flowed down to the Gulf of Mexico (Canal Corridor Association, 2009). Situated on the Chicago & Rock Island rail line was the small farming town of New Lenox, named after Lenox, Madison County, New York (Marcus, 2005).

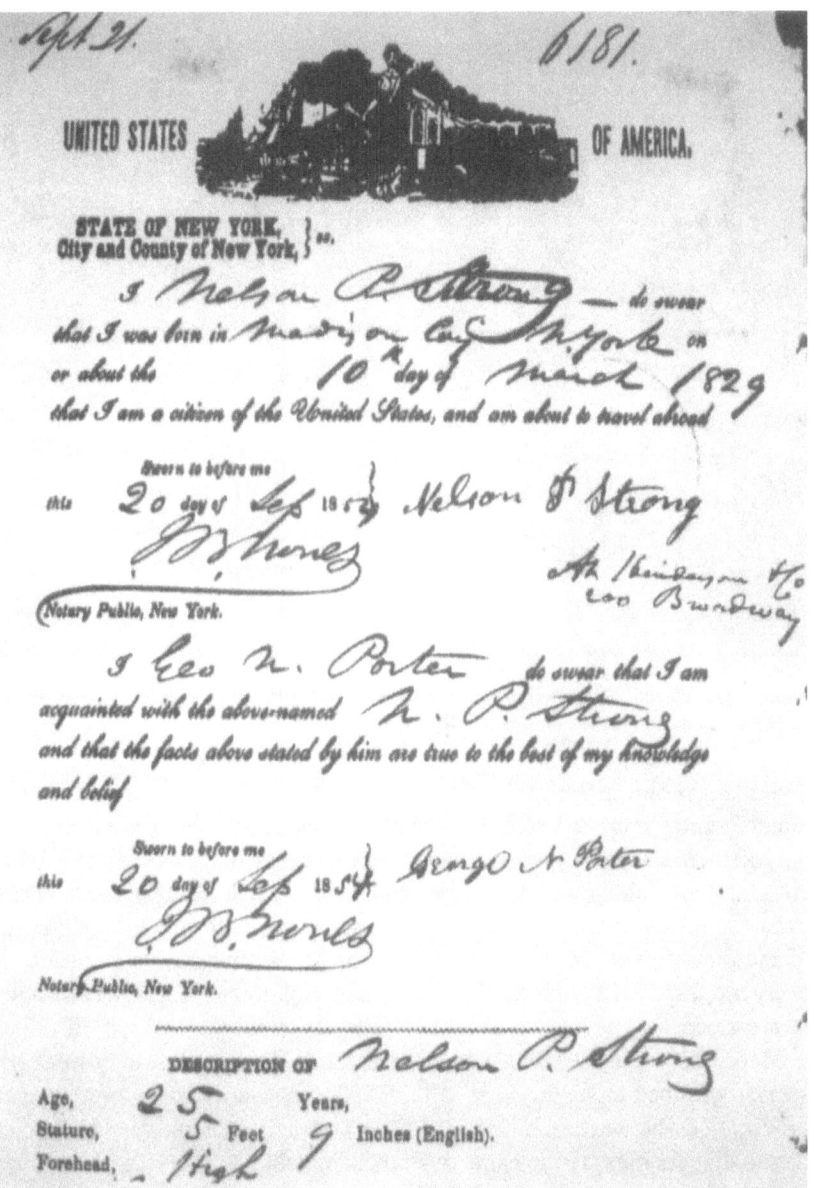

Photo 15.2 Nelson Philester Strong's 1854 passport application. He used his middle name instead of his first. *Courtesy www.ancestry.com.*

Photo 15.3 Twenty-first-century view of the Drake and William Selleck farm, Ingalls Corners Road, Perryville. *Author's collection.*

Sometime during the 1850s, Van left southern Wisconsin and moved some hundred miles south to live in Plainfield, Illinois, near his sisters and closer to his Mitchell cousins. Plainfield had its fair share of former Madison County emigrants and, along with them, the news they brought from back east. These updates and the letters Lydia and Ada exchanged with the New York part of the family were the only way for the Strong siblings to keep current on everyone, especially their aging parents and grandfather, and Otis, who was now sixteen.

Mary, the youngest sister, had since reached the age of twenty-three and seemed destined to stay in Perryville. While they were forging new lives on the frontier, she was teaching in the little Perryville school, soon to be married to a gentleman by the name of Francis Mead.

By 1854, oldest brother Nelson Philester Strong had gotten himself a U.S. passport and sailed to France with a friend. Two years later, while still in France, Philester married Mary Johnson. In 1860, he returned to America with his wife and their little girl, Lucinda Mary, named after two of his sisters.

Meet the Strong Family 113

This letter of February 1861 from Lydia Ann Strong of Joliet, Illinois, to her mother, Lydia Ann Strong of Perryville, New York, introduces us to the Strong family—she mentions every single member. The letter tells the story of the girls' everyday, simple life in Illinois and what America was like in the mid-nineteenth century. At the time she wrote this letter, Lydia was twenty-nine, Ada twenty-six, and Van thirty-one—none married. Lydia mentions how much she appreciated the modern conveyances that were lacking in Perryville that helped her get around easily. It was also clear that she thought of home often and missed her family she had left behind.

Chapter 16:

Lydia Writes Home

Joliet February 16th 1861
My Dear Mother
 I regret deeply that I am not more handy with writing but it does seem that I do what I can do to write well. One thing is that I wanted to go to Plainfield and hear from home. In that way I went up to Plainfield one week ago last Monday stayed until Saturday. I had a first rate time. Ada was very well but had been afflicted with a talon on her forefinger on her right hand. I had an excellent visit while gon. I visited Mr. Robertsons folks Mrs. Morrison, Mr. Hamilton. The Old Mrs Hemlin, Parnel, Mrs. Ranson send their best love to you all. They want to be particularly remembered in my letters home. Mother, Parnel gave Van and Ada their apples and saved the hardest ones for me so it would keep until I came up there. After I got there she went and got it—it was most all decayed except a strip on one side, which was good. She brought some Plums which were good. I am a thousand times obliged to you for your love and kindness. I felt like weeping when I received them, to think you were so thoughtful. Van is shelling corn doing good business at present I believe.
 My health is very good. I sew for a living this winter by the day, have 50 cts per day. I have sewed most of the time since school is out. Sewing has been easier for me this winter than teaching. I have succeeded by constant exertion & patient industry to have some money out at interest besides having desireable oweing to me all which is in safe hands. But I am so lonely since Ada left that my money is not much satisfaction. I have a very pleasant home this winter. I make it my home to Mr. Godards in Joliet, they are very kind to me. We have excellent meetings, & I attend the Sociable in town which are pleasant, but as I grow older I grow more stingy so I do not buy as many dresses as I ought too. I am glad Mary can go to school this winter & am glad to hear that your health is good. Parnel said you were fleshier than you used to be, but so I think you must have a great deal of care now Grandfather is sick, but it seems hard

to think he must go after living so many years without being prepared for that never ending Eternity. O that I could be the means of converting many souls, and doing much good in the wourld. I have often thought of Father for the last year, knowing that he is getting along in years, and I have felt deeply for his souls Salvation. Mother, I am glad to hear that Philester is coming home when his time is out. Oh that that time would come quickly. I wish I could make a visit at home I would have a good time . . . and I could then talk over many things, which would take time to write. I like this western country so well that I should not be satisfied to live there because here we have public conveyances to get around which I am deprived of there. I would like to see you all, but can not see that it is best to spend the money at present for visiting. give my love to Father Otis and all enquiring friends and accept a large share for yourself and all write soon. Direct to Joliet the same as ever

*From your affectionate daughter
Lydia A Strong*

There is so much to learn and think about in this one letter from a daughter on the prairie to her mother back east. Illinois was considered the west, small groups of people from eastern communities emigrated west together to form new towns, school teachers lived with families in their community, a thirty-mile trip from one town to another was a special event, young people went to sociables for entertainment and to meet people, and family members worried about the salvation of the nonbeliever.

It appeared from Lydia's letter that Van was making a good living, settled in Plainfield near her and Ada, with his six Mitchell cousins and Uncle Nash and Aunt Julia some fifty miles north, near Chicago. Ada had even moved the thirty miles from Joliet to Plainfield to be nearer to him and the other former New Yorkers from Madison County. Van worked a good stretch of land that he owned and farmed—that is, he owned it with help from a bank mortgage.

When the old decade of the 1850s came to a close and the new decade arrived, things started to change dramatically. There was an escalating tension and discontent brewing throughout the nation and unsettling talk about the new states west of Illinois entering the Union. Questions about the rights of states to decide their own laws had heated up over the issue of slavery. To many people in the South, loyalty to your state came before loyalty to your country, and they were fiercely opposed to being told what to do by the federals in Washington.

To rile things up even more, Abraham Lincoln, a favorite son of Illinois, surprised everyone by getting elected President of the United States. He already had the deck stacked against him when he took office in March 1861.

He was a Northerner, had little government experience, and he was a Republican, the anti-slavery party that wanted to contain slavery from spreading to the new states and territories, and some, the abolitionists, wanted to abolish it altogether. While the Republicans had support in the North, being a Northerner was not synonymous with opposing slavery.

While in his March 4, 1861, inaugural address Lincoln assured the slaveholding states that he did not intend to abolish slavery, even though he thought it a barbaric practice, slave states were not pleased with his election and his steadfast determination to keep the United States together. He stated emphatically, so the Southern states would take notice, "I have no purpose, directly or indirectly, to interfere with the institution of slavery in the States where it exists. I believe I have no lawful right to do so, and I have no inclination to do so . . . Those who nominated and elected me did so with full knowledge that I had made this, and many similar declarations, and had never recanted them."

They were not reassured by his words.

It was at this point in time that Van's simple life near his sisters as a farmer in this fertile prairie land took an unexpected and horrifying turn. He was not the only one whose whole world was upended. Not by a long shot. It was the spring of 1861, and the unthinkable had happened.

One after another, the Southern slave states seceded and joined a new country—the newly-formed Confederate States of America. Then, in April, South Carolina attacked and captured Fort Sumter, a Federal fort off the coast of Charleston. America was propelled into war with itself, North against South. At this time, the U.S. Army was a mere 16,000 men, most scattered at frontier posts further out west, and one third of the officers were from the South; most would remain loyal to their state and their Southern traditions and choose secession over their country (McPherson, 2008, pp.10–11).

A new story soon unfolded, one that concerned itself with unthinkable challenges and hardships. Each of Van's letters says enough to generate a score of questions and quests. The story of Van R. Strong, once an anonymous Civil War soldier, one of thousands from Illinois and millions from the country, teaches us about life during a momentous period of American history as no textbook could.

The letter from Lydia and the ones that follow in Part 2 from her brothers, Van and Otis, and her cousin, Charles, provide valuable pieces of information, clues, facts, personal perspectives, and ultimately an authentic window into their daily lives. With the help of quality primary and secondary sources, I learned their story and the rich issues, influences, and circumstances the country's citizens and soldiers faced during the Civil War:

- Perspectives of the North and South
- Homestead Acts
- The Soldiers–Regular Army, Volunteers, Veterans, and Draftees
- Enlistment, swearing in, furloughs, and mustering out
- Organization of a military unit—Corps, Wing, Divisions, Brigade, Regiment, Battalion, and Companies
- Transportation
- The role of women and freed slaves
- Army camp life and picket duty
- Early photography
- History of three Illinois and one New York Volunteer Infantry Regiments
- Maps and geography
- Chronology of the war
- Military weapons and battle strategies
- Details of the Battles of Fort Donelson, Shiloh (Pittsburg Landing), the sieges of Vicksburg and Petersburg
- Casualties of the war—deaths, wounded, missing, ill
- Army hospitals, diseases, and medical care in the Civil War

Photo 16.1   Falmouth, Virginia. Group in front of post office tent at Army of the Potomac headquarters, April 1863. *Courtesy of the Library of Congress, Prints and Photographs Division, Civil War Photographs [reproduction number LC-DIG-cwpb-03803].*

- Food rations, sanitation issues, living conditions
- The Prisoner Parole System
- Desertion and the role of provost marshal
- Lincoln's role as Commander-in-Chief
- The Presidential election of 1864
- And most notably, the importance of letter writing

As you read Van's letters and life story, think about all that had to be researched and understood to present an accurate picture of his life and the circumstances of the Civil War. Consider the range of pertinent primary sources available to me, and how I needed to use historical thinking to develop empathy, find evidence, and apply cause and effect to make sense of the information I found. Think about the rich content learned and the concepts and essential understandings that evolved from my quest.

Enjoy the human story that came together, one that wove actual personal experiences and feelings with universal enduring themes. And, finally, imagine the profound connections and intellectual challenges awaiting you and your students as you explore and analyze primary sources and breathe life into history.

Part Two

History Comes to Life

Chapter 17

Van's Story—From Farmer to Fighter

Plainfield IL 1861
Dear Mother
   Once more I take my pen in hand to write a few lines to you I wrote one letter to you before and got no answer from you I saw the Girls last week they was well then they are both well they are in Joliet now summer I am whare I was last week but am a going away from here soon I have been looking for a letter from Lest for some time I will look for two week more and give up if I could get some help by that time I can save my property that I have they is a mortgage on all I have got and if it is sold I can do nothing here but to go to the war that is all that I can do if I should go Mother don't feel bad nor hard about my going and now let me say to you here I have enlisted to go in the riffle company under Co Wilson at geneve the regiment is to go to lewisvill kentuck they will start in 2 or 3 weeks and unless I can get some money so to save my property I shall be sworn in to the servis and go with them but if you get this I will get your letter before I am sworn I will wait for your letter to come if you write soon as you get this so don't wait to long before you write and direct your letter to Plainfield Will co Ill my health is not first rate tell Mary Father to write to me my respects to you all so good knight

Van R. Strong

   I am a soldier. I should have liked to hear from Mother or Philester in time. But I did not and lost my mortgaged land to the bank. I was off to war as I had warned. In September 1861 I enlisted in the United States Army. I accepted my fate like a man, like father and grandfather and great-grandfather would have wanted. But losing my farm pained me, and I vowed I would return and start all over again, this time with a soldier's bounty.
   It was strange how things turned out. Here I was a soldier, like Great-Grandfather Noah Strong. Eighty years after he fought to free the American

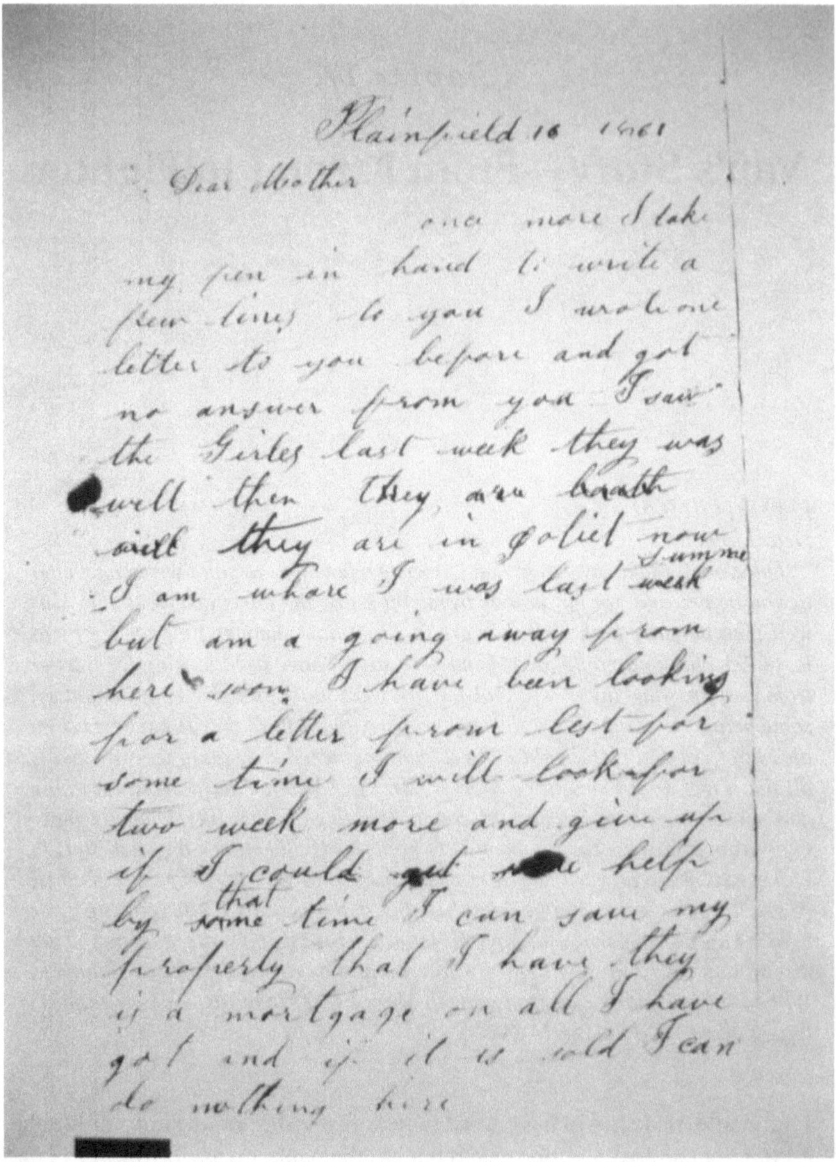

Photo 17.1 Copy of the first of Van's letters written in 1861 to his mother Lydia Ann Strong. *Author's collection.*

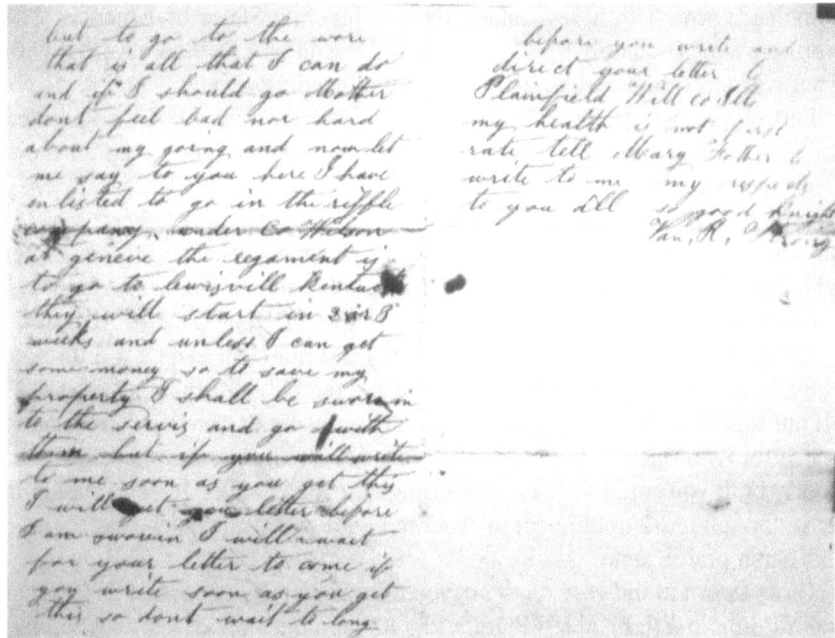

Photo 17.1 *(Continued).*

colonies from King George, I was trying to help preserve the union of those same colonies. How could it be? How could we be fighting our own brothers? The blame fell on those Southern Rebels who dared to break these United States apart. We were free from England, yet not a unified nation.

My good-byes to Ada and Lydia Ann were a rushed occasion. The girls met me at the Joliet train station as I passed through in late September. I was on my way to join up with a regiment in Camp Butler. Butler was further south of Plainfield, just outside of Springfield, where President Lincoln lived.

Putting down the rebellion that started in April at Fort Sumter was not going as well as the President expected. The Federal army had suffered badly at the Battle of Bull Run with the Rebs now camped in Manassas, just a short twenty-five miles from our nation's capital. But we all thought it just a temporary setback that the Union boys would soon reverse.

There wasn't much of a United States Army to work with, just a small force of career soldiers and officers who graduated from the West Point Military Academy. These officers were Northerners and Southerners who served side-by-side and were never meant to fight against each other. They each had to choose a side, North or South, and the tug toward their home state was strong. On account of this loyalty, many left the U.S. Army to fight for their Southern homeland, now with a new name, the Confederate States of America. The Northern states had only small militias, and President Lincoln knew that with what was left of the regular army, we would need more men.

Fort Sumter was in Rebel hands. The war was now real. Mr. Lincoln asked for 75,000 Union men to volunteer for the army, and then soon called for thousands more. I decided to be one of them and took a three-year enlistment. They no longer offered the optimistic three-month enlistment period. Other Plainfield boys and those of surrounding towns did the same and headed to Camp Butler with me. We were mostly a bunch of farmers, but unlike me, many also were leaving their lives as husbands and fathers to join the United States Army.

Camp Butler was a sea of humanity that did not even exist a month ago. Now there were 5,000 men here, more people than I had seen in my entire life all put together. What a sight it was, both confusing and exciting. The camp was a thrown-together town of paper-thin huts with wooden plank walls so poorly built you could see daylight through the many joints. It was a shelter at least, though it did not protect us from the wild winds and snow that plagued this harsh prairie state.

I was sworn in the very day I arrived, September 26, 1861, just as summer was turning to fall. I had left Plainfield with precious little of my own belongings. I knew I would have to carry what I brought, so I resisted taking much. What I could not take, I gave to the girls to keep until I returned. All I had stashed in my sack was some undergarments, paper and writing implements, a few dollars, and my pocketknife.

I also tossed in my straight razor and bar soap, along with a small metal mirror. My mustache and beard were full as was common for the times, and that suited me just fine. It didn't really give me much need for shaving utensils, although the army did have their rules and wanted you to look properly cared for. It was a fact they had rules for everything and a thick book to prove it. I thought as I was readying to leave for the war, what if I wanted to court a woman? I needed to look my most presentable, and the razor could come in handy if she preferred me clean-shaven. I had no idea what war would bring. Maybe it would bring a wife.

REVISED REGULATIONS Uniform, Dress, and Horse Equipments. 1862.

Article LI. The hair to be short; the beard to be worn at the pleasure of the individual; but, when worn, to be kept short and neatly trimmed.

Revised United States Army regulations of 1861, with an appendix containing the changed and laws affecting Army regulations and Articles of war to June 25, 1863, Page 462

Figure 17.1 Regulations on hair and beards from *Revised United States Army Regulations 1861 With an Appendix*, June 25, 1863. *Courtesy of Cornell University Library, Making of America Digital Collection.*

I counted on the United States Army to give me and the other boys all we needed to get by day-to-day as we served the country. I was dead sure they would because this was the Federal government. We could surely count on them. Everyone was saying this fight of Southern secession would be a short one and that the North had plentiful men and provisions to work with to bring them back around. The talk around camp and in the few newspapers we saw on occasion was that once us Yanks showed up in their cornfields and on their doorsteps, we would do the work asked by our President and end this war. We would bring the Rebs back to the Union, kicking and screaming if we had to, and with the money I earned, I would soon find myself back farming in the peaceful life I had planned.

The men wandering the camp were an odd-looking bunch, all shapes and sizes in all kinds of clothes, from tattered to respectable. As for me, I was thirty-one years old and feeling it, and I swear some of those boys were years younger than Otis—eleven or twelve at the most. I hoped young Oat would resist any such notion to run off to war.

I wanted to shoo those foolish little soldier boys back home to their mothers where they belonged. But if the army wanted them, I guess it was their right to serve. Maybe they would wash our clothes and make us coffee and leave the soldiering to us men. Or they could beat the drum and play the bugle if they were so talented. They could play taps at night to settle us down and reveille to rustle us up each morning. Otherwise, for my way of thinking, they ought to go home and grow up some before they took to soldiering.

Things moved fast at Camp Butler. New men showed up each day, and when there were enough of them, we formed a regiment. I wore my blue uniform coat the day I was sworn into Company I of the 46th Illinois Volunteer Infantry Regiment of the United States Army. I was made a corporal, a nice surprise at that. Mostly, you started out as private, the lowest rank in the army, so I thought this an honor. Must have been my age that made them think I could handle the extra responsibility. I was not sure about the extra responsibility, but I did like the extra dollar a month over the $13 privates were paid.

I discovered my cousin Charles Mitchell had volunteered up in McHenry County and was now in the 15th Illinois Volunteer Infantry Regiment. We enlisted on just about the same day, and it turned out our time in the army was to take just about the same path. From New York, to Illinois, and now we were both going to war together.

We had short time to practice being soldiers before we were ordered south to Fort Donelson. The Army of the Tennessee was waiting for more men. Few of us had ever been to Tennessee before, so we were curious about what Southern land and people were like. I had never seen what they called a plantation or slaves.

After a few weeks of drilling from morning to night, we were pretty good at setting up camp tents, digging trenches, shooting our muskets, and grinding and roasting coffee beans to boil our coffee. And we were real good at doing what we were told. Yep, Corporal Van R. Strong aimed to do his family proud as a soldier in the U.S. Army, and that meant obeying orders. There was no place in the army for a stubborn or questioning mind. So I vowed to put all such notions out of my head for the duration and get along.

We were restless. The boys were satisfied to finally head south to where the fighting was. Small fights between the blue and gray were flaring up in different states, and if we had to be in this army, we were aching to get on with it. Us Will County boys were afraid we would be too late for the fighting. Perhaps you find it strange that once we set our minds to it, there was no dampening our will to serve.

We got on the train to Cairo, and on February 11th the 46th Illinois and thousands of other soldiers sailed down the Ohio, Tennessee, and Cumberland Rivers to Fort Donelson. We were on a beauty of a boat, the steamship Belle Memphis, just two years old, headed to capture a Rebel fort. This boat ride was another new experience for me, but we were all crowded together, so I did not get to enjoy the opportunity as I would have liked.

It was still the deep winter up north, and we all expected the weather to be warmer in the South. That was what we had always heard, that the South was pleasant with mild weather and fertile land. Maybe we were not south enough because that was not the case in Tennessee when we arrived during the winter of 1862. It had been sunny and agreeable as we neared Donelson, and it was snowing by the time we got off the boat and marched to duty. That very first night I learned a hard lesson about being a soldier.

They put us to work standing guard of the general's headquarters with nothing to keep us warm from the cold and snow but what we were wearing. And we were not wearing much when we got off the Belle Memphis. There was no time to think of bad weather as we were herded into company formation. We did as told and dumped our extra gear at camp. Without our coats or blankets, we pretty near froze to death that night. You might say this was the beginning of my troubles.

The next day was my first taste of the fighting side of war. The rebels charged at us with a piercing yell, and we yelled "Hurrah" back at them and charged forward as commanded. The 46th lost a man that day, with two more wounded who I heard since died. Our Regiment was luckier than others who suffered many casualties. I had seen the elephant.

If I thought the war would be a swift rout for the Union and that the U.S. Army would take good care of its fighting men, then I was not well-informed. Nor were the other soldiers in Company I, as we were all confounded at the conditions we were made to bear. Even with victory, what we got at Donelson was a taste of death and poor conditions all around. If this was what it meant to be a soldier, I questioned whether an old man like me was cut out for a soldier's way of life. I was not used to such long marching and fighting with no sleep, no shelter over our heads no matter the weather, and not enough to eat.

There were thousands of troops at Donelson, both North and South, and we showed them pretty good what us Northern boys could do. We beat the rebels into surrender with help from a first-rate commander by the name of Ulysses S. Grant. Grant was a general in the regular U.S. Army. I thought it amusing that here was an educated man and graduate of the West Point Military Academy leading a rag-tag bunch of country boy volunteers who a few months ago were just regular farmers and laborers, not skilled in army ways. He seemed happy to have us, and we were proud to serve under him. We pledged to do him and the folks back home proud, and Uncle Abe, too.

Thanks to Grant and the victory at Donelson under our belts, we got renewed hope that the Union would prevail and make short shrift of this rebellion. Camp was buzzing about how General U. S. Grant had stood up to the South with a tightly clenched fist. A white flag and bugle call alerted the General that the confederates were surrendering Fort Donelson. The note the

Photo 17.2 View from lower river batteries pointing toward the Cumberland River, Fort Donelson, Tennessee. Battle of February 1862 was Van's first fight and Union's first victory. *Photo courtesy of Courtesy of Richard Edling, www.civilwaralbum.com.*

rebel courier boy carried stated that confederate General Buckner would surrender, but first they wanted the Union to give them some concessions.

We thought that a bold request, as they were not the victors and should be happy their lives had been spared. To our thinking, we needed to teach those Rebels the lesson that cutting ties with their mother country was not the easy job they might have thought. Grant turned out to be the man to do it. He was not inclined to make any such bargains with Southern commanders.

The couriers raced their horses back through the woods to deliver his answer. The defeated generals waiting at the fort read Grant's firm reply: unconditional surrender and nothing less. Our boys made cheers and hurrahs when we heard of Grant's stand. Why give those rebels anything was the sentiment in our company. It was because of them we were in this war far from home, hungry, tired, and losing our friends to Southern bullets. Now U. S. Grant was proudly known as Unconditional Surrender Grant, and we loved him dearly.

Right after capturing Donelson, they had us stand guard over the rebel prisoners. There were thousands of them. We did this for many days and nights straight through. We marched on foot up river to Fort Henry, the Rebs in tow. The Union Army had captured Fort Henry some ten days earlier, and I found a surprise waiting for me there. I discovered the 15th Illinois Volunteer Infantry Regiment was with our battalion. I was to be fighting alongside cousin Charles Mitchell in this western campaign. I would have looked to find him as soon as we arrived, but the captain had other things in mind for us to do. We stood guard again and then prepared to move on. Probably would have been of no use anyway. There were tens of thousands of soldiers, so finding him was a long shot.

We captured so many Confederate prisoners in these two battles, some say 12,000 of them, the army had to send 2,000 north to Camp Butler, the very Union camp we had just left. It was one of the few places large enough to house them. We got into this war so fast, I can't imagine the army even had time to think to plan for prisoners. The rebellion was supposed to be over in a few weeks. I thought of those drafty cabins and wondered how the Southern boys would take the Northern winter with the prairie winds blowing day after day. I am sure they were wondering, too, but more likely about how they would be treated in the hands of their enemy.

A fiery hatred raged between us and the Rebels, yet deep down many felt we were all still Americans. These Donelson and Fort Henry rebels were some of the first prisoners of the war, so everyone, North and South, was watching. This Civil War was new to us, and we did not yet know how our fellow countrymen would treat each other. When they arrived at Camp Butler, the able ones were put to work building a stockade and hospital. They lived in the same barracks as us and soon faced the same sanitation, disease, and ration problems we did in the field.

Van's Story—From Farmer to Fighter 131

The Donelson Rebs were squared away up north at Camp Butler and at other camps, no longer able to fight us. Our regiment moved on and joined what looked to be at least one hundred boats. We slowly made our way down the Tennessee River to Pittsburg Landing.

What a sight we made! I thought it a miracle that we failed to run into each other and sink our own boats, as we came close to doing so many times. Company I was on the steamship Aurora. We hadn't had much sleep since we left Butler, and rations were short and clean water scarce. A slow boat ride was alright by me and the other boys. Except for the ones who took ill.

I was hoping to have the two weeks to rest up, for it was my bad luck to get the ague at Donelson. Now I suffered with chills and fever and did not feel first rate. I was not the only one of the boys sick with malaria. I hoped this Pittsburg Landing was a regular town where we could get off the boats and get some good food and clean water to drink, and maybe even post a letter. That Tennessee River water, while pretty to float on, was making many a soldier sick with dysentery, and now I counted myself among that group. On top of the ague, this Tennessee two-step was wearing me out to where I feared I would soon be of little use to the army. I might just rather lay down and die right then and there.

Down the river close to Pittsburg Landing, we stopped on shore at Savannah. We were glad for the change of pace. When we got off the boat, I took this chance to visit with Captain Edward McAllister at his quarters. Edward was a good neighbor friend from Plainfield, same age as me, and a farmer, too. He could tell right away that his Plainfield boys were homesick and not happy with the army or our company officer. I told him so right out that the captain of Company I had proved himself to be weak and a coward at Donelson. He turned his back and ran away from the fight, leaving us there with no one to lead us. We had no respect for him, and he resigned and left camp right after Donelson was surrendered.

McAllister listened to my complaints but would have none of it. Not even when I told him the boys wished they had signed on to his artillery regiment instead. We knew McAllister was honorable and would treat us better than the last one. Captain McAllister sent me off with little sympathy and a good deal of ribbing, telling me we should have known better than to sign up in that sorry excuse for a man's company. It was then I truly realized that I was in the army and my life was no longer in my control. Complaining did not get you very far, even if you knew a captain. I feared things were only going to get worse.

What happened next I must sincerely say, I was not, nor never could be, prepared for. 60,000 Federals met 40,000 Confederates cannon to cannon, musket-to-musket, for two bloody days that could only be imagined in the most feverish of a nightmare.

Chapter 17

Instead of a chance to rest up and get over my ailments, after we landed and set up camp, the Battle of Pittsburg Landing soon commenced. It happened not far from the landing itself and was a surprise, at that. We were intending to fight the Rebels on our own terms at Corinth down in Mississippi. That was some twenty miles south where the railroads crossed. We didn't know the Secesh had already snuck up from Mississippi to Tennessee to meet us where we landed, determined to fight on their terms.

That day in April 1862, we heard the hair-raising Rebel yell once again, and before we knew what happened, 24,000 men died in forty-eight hours.

New House of Reffuge July 1/62
Dear Brother,
I now seat myself to write a few lines to say for the first time I hope you will forgive me for not writing you before and I don't feel much like writing you a very long letter on account of my health is so poor. I have not seen a well day for over 4 monts. I was taken sick soon after the donelson fight I had a hard time thare after they surrendered the fort the 10 of febuary our regament was taken to gard the prisoners we marched three miles that morning before we was poot on gard it was nine oclock in the morning and kept thare till 3 the next day without being releaved then marched till sundown and camped with not mutch to eat this was on the eve of the 17 of Feb the 16 we started with one small peace of meat and 2 hard crackers on the 16 our officers could not get any for us so we looked out for our selves we went to whare the commissaries stuff was and found tea rice and sugar it didn't take long to open them and get what we wanted we boiled our tea and rice then picked in shugar went free it was nice white sugar

The 18 morning came the Col sent someone to the landing before he would leave for some thing to eat it came about noon on the 19 we reached Ft henry than stayed a few days then was ordered to pitts Burg landing was on the boat 2 weeks going up the river they was over 100 boats in the fleat then landed and camped ½ mile in from the landing we staid thare till after the battle our regt went into the engagement 2 Oclock in the morning on the 6 was in all day in the fight the next morning we was ordered out on the right wing I went with them till after we had drove them back 1 mile then we was oblige to retreat the same ground and could not stand it any longer the Lieutenant Col told me to go back to the camp I started back did not get back till four in the afternoon 2 miles on the account of being sick I had a hard shake of the ague and fever all night it rained all night to we had to lay on our arms and take it not much fun at that so you can see that they is not mutch fun in soulderin

I have been in the hospitaal for the last 2 monts for the last 3 days I have stuck to my bed the most of my time but now better this morning I have the cronic direrear rheumatism week back and my lungs is a fected the—the that I take now is helping me. Now Oat I must clos for I am tired out show this letter to Wm Selleck tell him to write me Oat write soon as you get this dont poot it off a day thinking it will do just as well at it at once for I want to here from home give my love to Father Mother Sister Moly and F. M. direct your letter just as it is on this other peace of paper give my love to all good by for the time

From Van R Strong To Oatis R Strong

Tell mary I have not forgot her tell her and to write I should like to have her husband write to

Yours with respect

It pained me to think back to the battle, and it took many months before I could write this letter to Otis. I had some of my strength back and wanted to tell him what the war was really like. The Rebs called it Shiloh, we called it Pittsburg Landing, but they were just different names for the same hell of a battle. My regiment suffered some 160 casualties at Pittsburg Landing, a sacrifice they made for what those in Washington claimed was a Union victory, a much-needed one at that. The cruel truth was Shiloh means "place of peace."

It was a slim victory. Luck was barely with us as Grant's Army of the Tennessee finally beat the Rebels back. I am sure our President was most relieved to receive the report of our success. Maybe then the North's defeat last summer at Bull Run would no longer be the rallying cry to the Confederates. News of the massive loss of life on both sides at Pittsburg—24,000 killed, wounded, or missing—had a sobering effect on the country no matter where you lived. To us that were there, we could not call it a victory for either side.

I did not last long after the battle. With chronic diarrhea and the ague I was neither fit nor interested in soldiering. I was of little help as the men of Grant's army buried our Union dead, Rebs, too, in mass graves near the Shiloh church. With the dead buried, they gathered up the horribly sick and wounded and laid them on wagons. They marched the rest of us the twenty miles south to Corinth, and my infirmity caused me much discomfort. I had to stop many times along the way.

Corinth was where we were headed to in the first place before the Rebs surprised us. Now we could seize those two intersecting railroads and squeeze the Southern boys out of the area. The rails would be a big help for the Union to send supplies to our army in the South. We were already in strong need of munitions and rations and medicine, too. And it would have been nice to have shoes and clothes that did not fall apart. What we were issued back in Butler was of cheap material. Merchants had made fools of the government by promising delivery of the thousands of uniforms they needed in a hurry. If the war lasted only three months as thought, the shoddy goods might have done the job.

We finally reached Corinth in early May. Those Rebs pulled back until they turned tail and retreated without much fight. They fled across the bridge and scattered. It was a good show for the Regiment with few casualties this

Chapter 17

time, and one near broke my heart. Our Captain Davis, as good an army man and leader as you could hope to see, fell mortally wounded in this battle. The poor soul was still recovering from wounds he got at Shiloh, and then was lost to this earthly world for good.

There was another casualty I could not ignore, although I sincerely tried. I was still not feeling first-rate. I battled the dysentery more than I did the Rebs. The heat and fatigue further strained my weak condition until I was so ill they sent me to the field hospital in Hamburg, way back up in Tennessee. Before long, the lieutenant figured I would not be returning to the battlefield any time soon. He sent me and the other sick soldiers to the New House of Refuge Army Hospital over by St. Louis. Missouri was said to be one of those officially neutral states, but the people were not neutral as far as we could tell. They held strong opinions on both sides of the issues. Union soldiers were both scorned and welcomed, and you never knew which greeting you would receive.

Perhaps you think I would have been glad to be in the hospital, where I was away from the fighting and could convalesce. This was not so. The New House of Refuge was a sad place to have such a hopeful name. There was not much refuge from pain there, and the place itself bred despondence. It was an unfriendly building that let in little daylight with nothing pleasant to look at, inside or out. I could not stand to think of the orphans and neglected children made to live their lives in this drab place, in this dirty city. They were detained against their will with no family to care for them. I was blessed growing up with my family in wide-open green spaces with beautiful land and clean water and healthy air to breathe. There was no fairness to life.

We were here against our will, too, but the truth was we would fare much worse if it were not for this place and the others like it. I do have to say we ate better here than with the regiment. No more slim daily ration of two chunks of hardtack and one piece of tired-looking and worse-tasting cured meat. At the hospital, we had fresh, roasted meat and hash and pudding, and even soft bread instead of hardtack. I had not seen such food since I was in Plainfield before this war started, and not much even then.

I wondered where those orphans were, now that the army had taken over their home for a hospital. We heard the army was taking houses and churches and any building they could for the wounded and sick of the war. I had seen that to be the case in Tennessee and Mississippi. Hospitals were now commonplace where none were needed before. The government was even forced to build large hospital buildings in Washington for all the casualties back east. We heard the Army of the Potomac was suffering hard the trials of war with mounting losses and little progress to show for it.

Sick and injured men were brought into our ward daily, and many left dead. They had the small pox and measles, terrible rashes of the skin with fever, and we prayed they did not spread it to the rest of us. They were quarantined at one end of the floor, separated only by curtains and thin partitions. Others arrived with horrible wounds wrapped with bloody cloth bandages that were nothing more than ripped shirts. The surgeons worked hard to save each man, and often it was a limb, not a life, that was lost. Amputation was the answer to saving many lives, and amputate they did. The sounds of men in pain echoed off the walls, day and night, and I never again in all my life wanted to smell ether or see a dieing man with his mind gone in fever.

This war had made a whole new obligation for the lady folk in St. Louis and Washington D.C., and small towns and country houses that got in the way of the fighting. They were volunteers, just like we were, kind nurses who cared for us like we were their own kin. I figured they hoped someone would do the same for their husbands and sons and brothers if they ever fell from injury or disease. Don't think the ladies and children who were at home did not help. They did in their own way, and we were appreciative of them. They made bandages for the army as they were always in short supply. They knit us socks, too, and even made some of the bullets we were shooting.

I gave thanks that I was one of the sick ones, not one wounded on the battlefield by the ripping blast of a musket minié ball or exploding cannon fodder. That minié ball bullet spun so fast and traveled so far it could kill at half a mile. And it was accurate, too. No one had ever seen anything like it. It made killing each other easier.

So far I had my head and gut and my limbs intact, though all were made weak by the ague, and I was prone to sleep more than was usual. I knew the U.S. Army would likely put me on half-duty somewhere until I could march and fight again, so as to not be a burden on my Regiment. It was all I was good for.

Lying there in bed gave me a lot of time to think. Maybe too much time, at that. A conflict grew inside me over how I felt about doing guard duty in camp, safe from the fighting, while my Regiment was in harm's way. But the Pittsburg battle was still with me every moment, awake or asleep, and now that I knew what war was like, I must admit I was not so anxious to return. As I rested on my bed in the New House of Refuge those many months, I could not chase those two days in April from my mind. The moaning of dieing soldiers next to me did much to remind me of the carnage on the battlefield. Those who were there will say they had seen more than any man should ever witness.

On that battlefield, I saw men not just already dead and dieing, I saw them alive one moment and struck dead by blasts the next, with body parts blown yards away so as not to know who was who. Scores at a time were sent to their maker. Sometimes they were not so blessed as to be killed out right, and instead lay in agony on the field, out of our reach to help them. Their moans and cries for water and their mothers are burned in my memory.

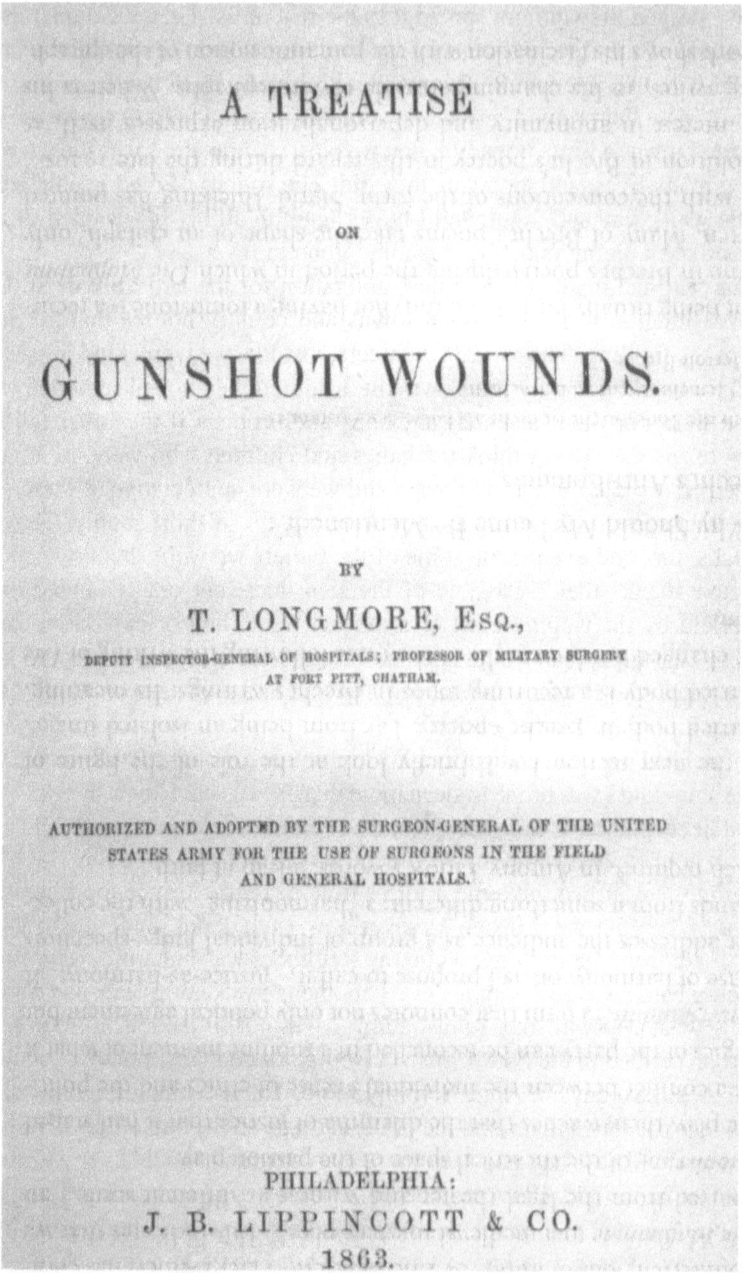

A TREATISE

ON

GUNSHOT WOUNDS.

BY

T. LONGMORE, Esq.,

DEPUTY INSPECTOR-GENERAL OF HOSPITALS; PROFESSOR OF MILITARY SURGERY
AT FORT PITT, CHATHAM.

AUTHORIZED AND ADOPTED BY THE SURGEON-GENERAL OF THE UNITED
STATES ARMY FOR THE USE OF SURGEONS IN THE FIELD
AND GENERAL HOSPITALS.

PHILADELPHIA:
J. B. LIPPINCOTT & CO.
1863.

Photo 17.3 Original 1863 Army medical manual: *Treatise on Gunshot Wounds*, by Longmore. Medical personnel faced the devastating wounds inflicted by the minié ball bullet. *Courtesy of Dr. Michael Echols, American Civil War Surgical Antiques.*

It was not just our boys in blue who cried out. Those Southern boys were no better off lying out there on the open field. With clothes and flesh shredded, one could not easily tell a Reb from a Federal, and I think it did not matter much. They were both dead and dying, having given their life for one cause or the other.

I had learned that bravery had no particular flag. Cousin Charles Mitchell would surely swear what I was saying was true, as his 15th IL Volunteers served with us when we fought at Shiloh Church to hold the line steady from the rebel attack.

When we mustered in that December day at Camp Butler, our regiment numbered near 1000. At Shiloh, the 46th Illinois lost many volunteers and officers, too. We were down to near 850. No one could question if Will County was doing its part to preserve the union. Our commander read us a fine dispatch from General Hurlburt himself that praised our conduct on the Shiloh battlefield. He called it noble that without food or sleep, we helped the army's Fighting Fourth Division hold the line. He told us to keep this act of bravery in mind to hand down to our children when we conquered a peace and went home to a gentile life once again.

Conquered a peace. He was right with that choice of words. It surely would take conquering, as nothing was coming easy in this war. We had conquered the place of peace, and we were still fighting. Maybe it was God's punishment for the killing we had done.

Come September '62, some five months after Shiloh, the army doctors finally found me fit to leave the hospital. We had heard word that if a soldier was taken sick and not recovered in two months, he would get a medical discharge and be sent home. This was not true in my case. The army must have needed us bad, for they waited five months for me to get healthy. I was still not first rate, though not sick enough to stay at the New House of Refuge. I had the constant coughing, the diarrhea, and overall weakness. I vowed to get healthy and never return there or to any place like it.

Like I figured, they shipped me south to serve half-duty detached detail at the Negro Department in Bolivar, Tennessee. What made this detail all the worse was I missed my company boys. For weeks, I did my best to be a good soldier, and that is the truth, so please believe it. I found myself thinking I could no longer stay on at Bolivar. I got by from day to day, but was not myself in either body or spirit. Maybe it was what happened at Pittsburg Landing or my lingering sickness that convinced me to do what I did next.

I am not proud to say, nor am I fully sorry either, that I gave into temptation and left my detail without permission. The partial pay we received gave me the means to do it. With money in my pocket, home was calling to me worse than ever, and it was my old home in New York that beckoned me. I wanted to be with all the loving people I had not seen for years. Some of the other boys felt the same, and we made a pact. We waited for a night when clouds covered the harvest moon and headed north.

Once we traveled a safe distance from camp, we stopped to make ourselves look less of a soldier. I took off my coat and folded it up in my knapsack. We walked a good deal on foot at first, listening for both Rebs and Union troops. Both were a danger to us now. We had many days of alert running and skirting the army to escape from secessionist Tennessee into friendly Kentucky. I was the only one headed to New York and went east by myself towards Ohio. I was determined to see Mother, Father, Mary and Frances Mead, and my dear brothers, Lester, who might have come home as promised, and young Otis, whom I missed most of all.

I felt like a runaway slave on the Underground Railroad I had heard tell about. Like a runaway slave, if I were caught, I would be returned and punished. I knew to steer clear of all the Federals around Maryland and Washington. Once I was far north enough in Ohio, and then in Pennsylvania, I used some of my pay to take the train to Syracuse and then Canastota, and walk to Perryville.

The government had not started drafting men into service yet, which helped me in my plot. It was not unusual to see an able bodied man of soldiering age in civilian clothes. None the less, I slept with one eye open the whole time, ready to run and jump off a moving train if need be. I did not know what a provost marshal would do if he caught me.

Walking up Ingalls Corners Road had my heart pounding. It felt good to be in such familiar territory and to see the Selleck farm and our house next door. There was both shock and joy on their faces when my folks saw me at the door. They were surprised past words at first, and then they turned scared. They could see I was not injured and wondered how I could be home with the war still raging. They came to the hard realization that I had got up and left. Deserted. They said it right out and told me they were afraid I would be hung or shot, and they would be, too, for harboring a deserter. I told them not to worry, for I heard the army was not executing soldiers who were absent without leave. If they did, it would be too much a loss. Men were deserting by large numbers every day, and the army could not afford to kill off a good number of their own fighting men.

Leaving the army without permission must have been even more tempting for the Rebs. They were close to home and knew their women folk and children were helpless when the Union Army marched through their states and fighting erupted. There was no fighting in New York, no armed Rebel forces wandering the countryside, ready to surprise and uproot folks at any moment. The truth be told, there was nothing to remind us of the war down South except the absence of our men and boys. The peace and quiet made soldiering and the horrors of Pittsburg Landing seem faraway and unreal.

I got myself caught up on the news and was saddened to hear that grandfather Lemeul had passed three months before. I should have liked to say good-bye. Lester had not come home as hoped, and my neighbor friend, Abram Van Dusen, had joined the army. I shared some stories of what the war was like and made sure Oat listened. He asked a host of questions, and I answered them honestly, even when the truth was hard to hear and even harder to say. I hoped my tales would knock sense into him and spare him the hell of soldiering. Oat was now seventeen and developing a mind of his own, and he had a loyal streak.

Fall in New York State was a most pleasant time, with maple and oak and poplar and birch leaves in blazing color and crops harvested and put up for the winter. I arrived in time to see the color of the leaves just before the November winds blew them dead to the ground. Mother made apple cider and corn bread, and we stewed a few chickens while I was there. I did my share of tilling fields and chopping and splitting firewood, and for the first time I could remember, I was content to be in Perryville, working Mr. Selleck's land. It felt good working side by side with young Oat, who had turned into a fine, strong man.

There was no telling how long my stay would be, so I kept busy each day to be of help to Mother and Father. The November skies were gray and gloomy, a sure sign that before long the family would need many cords of wood to fight off the cold. Winter came to Perryville, and we soon had days of snow and bitter wind. Since marrying, Mary and Francis had their own place not far away, and I went there and helped them. Mary was in good hands, for Francis was a skilled and hard-working man, a prosperous harness maker. Now married, she could no longer teach in the little school.

The days turned into weeks, and the weeks passed a month. I stayed close to home with my family. I tried not to draw much attention to myself and was still able to make the reacquaintance of some neighbors. We never talked about if I was staying or going back. All the time, I wondered if someone would turn me in.

We were content with this arrangement when one day there came a solid banging on the door. A provost marshal agent came to the house and settled the question for us. He asked my name and took me into U.S. Military Custody right then and there. I did not think it smart to protest, and just gathered up my knapsack and uniform, which Mother had kindly cleaned. In the name of the Provost Marshal of the United States Army, he ordered me back to my regiment. I wondered at the common sense of the army paying good money for someone to travel hundreds of miles to track down a couple of missing soldiers.

That provost marshal agent was cold to my predicament. I guess you need to be hardhearted to drag men back to war and their likely death. He was paid to do a job, and he did it.

> REVISED UNITED STATES ARMY REGULATIONS OF 1861.
> WITH AN APPENDIX CONTAINING THE
> CHANGES AND LAWS AFFECTING ARMY REGULATIONS AND
> ARTICLES OF WAR TO JUNE 25, 1863.
> WASHINGTON: GOVERNMENT PRINTING OFFICE.
> 1863.
> ARTICLE XII: REGIMENTS.
> "160. Rewards and expenses paid for apprehending a deserter will be set against his pay, when adjudged by a court-martial, or when he is restored to duty without trial on such condition."

Figure 17.2   1863 Union Army Regulations regarding deserters. Van's records show he was absent without leave and he paid for the services of the provost marshal. *Courtesy of Cornell University Library, Making of America Digital Collection.*

After many blessings for a safe return, I looked at Perryville and my family for what I hoped was not the last time. The marshal escorted me and a few other New York men on the train back to Tennessee. I told him I never intended to desert for good, and it was the honest truth. I knew my duty was with the U.S. Army, fighting to put the Union back together. Yet, each day in Perryville I would say, "Tomorrow, tomorrow I will head back south to Tennessee to find my regiment." And each day I could not tear myself away from the peace and kindnesses I found there among the rolling hills and my loved ones. I knew where I belonged. The rub was it was in two places, and the choice to be at home was not mine to make. Such was the predicament of a soldier in this war.

My leave, though worthwhile for my soul and overall health, was an expensive proposition. I spent much of my pay traveling north and helping Mother buy sugar and salt and other provisions she needed. On my return to the army, which I did without complaint, the government charged me for my transportation back south and the cost of the services of the provost marshal. I also lost pay for the two months I was gone.

I considered myself lucky. The regiment was in winter quarters, not set to fight any time soon. They must have been content to get me back, for I faced no physical punishment. No firing squad or thrashing. They did keep a close watch on me and kept me off picket duty for a long time, and I had to face military law. They took away my rank as a corporal and demoted me down to a private. It was a small price to pay for the time I got to spend in such a peaceful place. There were so many deserters that both the North and the South were at their wit's end to know what to do about us. If truth be known, had they executed deserters as the law permitted, we would never have tried it.

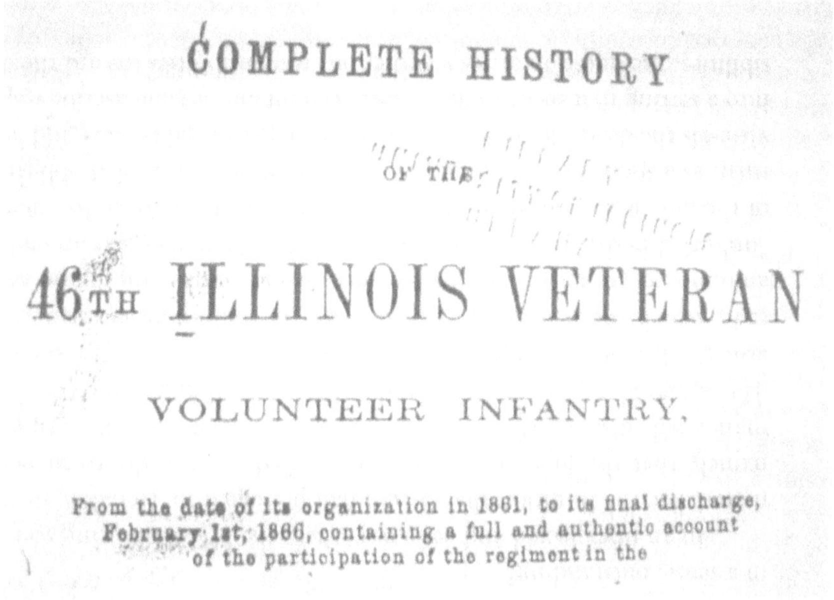

COMPLETE HISTORY

OF THE

46TH ILLINOIS VETERAN

VOLUNTEER INFANTRY.

From the date of its organization in 1861, to its final discharge, February 1st, 1866, containing a full and authentic account of the participation of the regiment in the

Photo 17.4 Cover of 1886 *Complete History of the 46th Illinois Veteran Volunteers. Author's collection.*

It was a large relief that the boys in Company I accepted me back as one of them, with no hard feelings that I could see. We lived in close quarters, and I would not like to have been the black sheep. It was now January 1863, and I had not seen them since Corinth in May of last year. They must have thought me dead or discharged. While I was situated elsewhere, they had been busy, not fighting battles so much as patrolling and skirmishing, trying to keep hold over the parts of Tennessee and Mississippi the Union had already captured. I joined them as they continued to do so. If you were to follow the news of the 46th, you would understand it when I say I soon knew more of these states than I did of both New York and Illinois.

Over the early months of this new year, we marched from one end of the region to the other. We snaked and circled in pursuit of rebel troops and their supply trains. It was on January 6 when cousin Charles Mitchell's 15th IL and my 46th IL escorted a large Union ammunition wagon train to Lagrange, Tennessee. After a long stretch at camp from mid-January though February 5, we marched back to Memphis, and then in April, we took an expedition to Hernando, just south of Memphis.

During all this criss-crossing, patrolling, and setting up camp, our generals were lying in wait for the right time to turn the siege of Vicksburg into a full attack. We all knew Vicksburg was one of the grand prizes of the war. Whoever held that river city on the hill controlled the mighty Mississippi River and all the ships and supplies that traveled it. Capturing Vicksburg would bring the end of the war closer, and we all wanted that.

No matter the duty, on the march or not, the days were long, long for different reasons. I do not know which I disliked more, the endless tramping though fields and woods tangled in thickets or ankle deep in sticky mud, or sitting in camp waiting. We fought the mosquitoes and diarrhea, and sometimes Reb guerillas. While holed up, we stood picket and drilled in the morning before it got too hot, then again late in the day. It tried our patience.

On account of all this extra time, our muskets were kept polished bright, clean, and ready to use. If there was water nearby, we washed our shirts and underwear. They had reading material for us, mostly about living a good, Christian life. Otherwise, with not much to do, we used our nit combs, wrote letters, whittled, and played cards and baseball to kill time. We had to be ready if we were called to fight, but it was less risky and unsettling than skirmishing with the Rebs in the countryside, or even worse, meeting them on the battlefield.

Our white tent cities rose up in the middle of nowhere, and the air was filled with smoke from hundreds of campfires. We were thankful to pitch our tents as when marching, we often slept in open air on damp ground with the rain pouring down on us. It was a wonder we all did not die from poor lungs and fever. We pitched row after row of two man pup tents, according to company. This made it easier to keep track of everyone, especially to keep a keen eye out for deserters. I figured they still had their sights on me, but I did not feel bad about it.

In no time flat, we could put together a tent camp so well-ordered that it looked like we had lived there for years. And in no time flat, we could take it down, gather our gear, hoist our cleaned and loaded muskets over our shoulders, and move on. Experience is a good teacher, especially in the army. I learned to be sure to have water in my canteen and a small piece of hardtack tucked in my haversack in case we had no rations. It happened regularly.

The boys put up large tents for the post office, chapel, and camp hospital. We also dug latrines. I'm the first to admit that these latrines were a luxury we enjoyed, especially on account of my ailments. We were mighty appreciative to have them and other small comforts that reminded us of home. There was always a sutler or two around, selling things we needed like toothbrushes and soap and underwear at high prices. They went with us from camp to camp as allowed by the army. They were the only supply store around and had us over a large barrel. They could charge what they wanted, and they did. Sutlers were businessmen and nothing more. They took no pity on us poor soldiers who hadn't been paid in months.

You could count on photographers following us. They took pictures of the aftermath of the battles and were eager to take our portraits, cartes de visite they called them. They were also eager to take our money. Hawking worked on many, as we were restless and bored, and it had been some time since most had seen our loved ones. The photographers tempted us with the promise that one such carte de visite would bring comfort to those who missed us. With our likeness to look at, they could keep happy thoughts of their beloved soldier. If we didn't bite, they appealed to our pride at being United State soldiers in Lincoln's army and to our vanity, telling us how fine and respectable we would be pictured in our uniforms.

This was all true, no doubt, but most of us had precious little money for such frivolity. We'd been paid but once since the day we enlisted, and that was partial. What little money we had was sent from home or won by

Photo 17.5 Cartes de Visite portraits of soldiers (and a lady friend) from the 8th Illinois Veteran Calvary, collected by soldier Joseph Willis Cook, and preserved by his family along with his original letters and other memorabilia. *Courtesy of the collection of Deb Moses.*

gambling. We used it for food and writing paper and stamps. I had used up most of my pay for my adventure north and had to make do.

Some enterprising souls like me made extra money whittling fancy wooden rings, walking sticks, and chess and checkers pieces. If all the boys who owed me paid for the rings I sold them, I would have had plenty of money for what I needed, like extra food if there was any to buy, and writing materials. Rations and letters kept us alive, and they were scarce.

The special appeal of camp life was the promise of a letter. This business of sending and getting letters was one of the hardest parts of soldiering, next to fighting and disease. It was usually more disappointment than reward. We wrote often since we never knew when we would get another chance or if this letter would be our last.

Mail call was the one thing that could interrupt a good game of cards, even if there was money riding on the outcome. The boys who could write wrote letters many times a month and some even a few a week, and then they commenced to wondering how many of those letters would make it to their destination and if we would ever get a letter in return. We puzzled at how the U.S. mail department could even track us down at all. We were more than a million soldiers scattered all over the South and on the move most days. It figures that during this time in camp, when we stayed put long enough for the postal couriers to find us, our hopes for a letter were high.

Don't doubt it when I say I saw many teary eyes when a soldier got a letter, and many when he did not. When no letters arrived, as was most often the case, our spirits sank low. The boys were overtaken by melancholy, and you would be, too, if day after day you left mail call empty handed. I, for one, know this to be true. For every few letters I wrote, I was most thankful if I got one in return, and months passed in between the writing and the receiving. I stooped to begging my family to write to me, and letters were still scarce. I did not rightly know if I should be angry at the United States Postal Service or my family. It was no wonder the boys drank all the whiskey they could find.

When not in camp, our division tramped the fields of Tennessee and Mississippi. Our regiment made progress in rousting the Rebels out of their strongholds. Rations were partial and we were starving. We took to eating berries and anything else we found that was fit to eat. If luck was with us, we picked up pigs and chickens to eat along the way.

There was not much real fighting. Lafayette, Memphis, and Hernando were secured. Yet, the Union had not yet been able to take that fortress on the hill. Vicksburg was still held by the Rebs as it stood watch over the Mississippi and all that moved in its waters. Without it, they said, we could not win the war. It was already past two years since the first cannon fire of this war, and victory did not appear to be in easy reach, as we had once believed it to be.

When the word came down from the generals that it was time for the siege of Vicksburg to move forward, we were glad to be doing something worthwhile. They told us U.S. Grant was in charge again, and he had a plan to take the city. I trusted that man who did right by us in Donelson and Pittsburg Landing.

> *Near St. Louis Sept.18/63*
> *Dear Mother,*
> *Once more I will try to let you no that I am well I have wrote you two letters since I left you and now as soon as you get this I want some of you to write without delay so that I may here from you and if you should not write for three or for days after you get this it may be to late for me to get it as they is no certenty of stay her any certin length of time I hope not long for I had rather be south with the army than here in the paroll camp we don't get a nuf to eat of rations we only draw ¾ rations and don't get near all of that the comsaries is in to mutch of a speculation but we can buy all that we want cheap for money that I have not got and don't now how soon we will be paid off. and I want you to give Lydia Ann this letter so that if she has not sent the money west I should like to send it to me if she can soon as she gets this and if it cant send it soon I don't want it sent here I would not wrote for it had I any or had a plenty to eat if she can send the money I want it poot in a letter*
> *Mother has Lest come home or did he say away if he has come tell him to come out here to see me that I was there to see him and spent all of the money that I had it just a pleasant journey to come here and see the country*
> *How is marary a getting a long is she well and Mr Mead give them my best respects and tell them to write to me have you herd from Adah if so how does she get along did she get to work in the factory how do Mr and Mrs Selleck folks get along tell them that I think of them every day and wish I could see them a little while tell them they have my best wishes tell Oat to be a good boy and keep his tobaco clean*
> *I must close my poor letter write soon as you get this and direct your letter the same as I do*
> *Good buy for this time*
>
> Van R. Strong
> Co I 9 [?]th Batalion
> Paroll Prisnors
> Benton Barracks
> St. Louis Mo

This war headed in strange and unexpected directions for both the country and for me. The news was not good from other battles. The Federals had still not stopped the secession. It was now the third year of the war, and I was presently held up in prisoner parole camp. It was the worst of places next to the battlefield and the army hospital, and, once again, it was a matter of being in the wrong place at the wrong time. Don't feel bad, though, as I was still alive and feeling first rate.

General Grant figured the only way to capture Vicksburg was to surround it. Not everyone agreed, including our President, but Grant had a certain stubbornness of mind and good instincts that the President respected.

Under orders, our Fighting Fourth Division moved to Young's Point on the 15th of May and then up the Yazoo River to Chickasaw Bayou. It was a wet deal for all involved. We got off the boats and waded across the deep swamp to the bluff. We had to hold our muskets up high over our heads as we walked. It was days before we dried out. We positioned ourselves to the right of Grant's army, and on orders, marched to Synder's Bluff. We continued toward Vicksburg to set ourselves in good position. We were ready to lend support when needed.

They saw fit to put me back on picket duty. I suppose I had proved myself trustworthy. Each company had picket duty every few days while the other boys back in camp kept ready to fight off an attack or to make one if the time was right. I cannot say I looked forward to standing guard in those dark woods, not able to see who or what was near, although it did break the monotony of camp life and waiting for something to happen.

On the night of the 25th of May, the boredom was broken for good. Five companies from our Regiment went out on picket duty as we were used to doing. We advanced to make a picket line on a ridge with a good vantage point.

Before we could even react and fire a shot, armed Rebels showed up from nowhere and surrounded the lot of us. In a moment's time, 104 soldiers and seven officers were captured. Some were able to run fast and escape capture. I was not one of them. I thought for sure these Rebs, with their wild yell, would turn their rifles on us right then and there.

They did not. I counted it as another surprise of this confounded war. They marched us to their camp in Vicksburg and held us there. They had the humanity to feed us, but the food we got was worse than what the U.S. army had been feeding us. It looked like Southern boys had less to work with than us Yanks.

We held fear of what the Rebs would do to us and were deeply relieved when, after a couple of days, they rounded us up and marched us to a meeting place. On the outskirts of the city, they handed us over to the U.S. Army unharmed and no worse for our captivity. I had heard of paroles and trades of prisoners between the North and South, but I did not believe this really happened. On the battlefield, we feared for our lives at the hands of an enemy who hated us so much. As a prisoner of war, we had no reason to fear them less. Yet the North and South traded prisoners without incident in a show of honor and fairness.

Though in Union hands, we were not returned to our division as we thought would happen. Instead, Federal marshals took us to a Union parole camp in St. Louis. I could not believe I was back in that city again. We reported to Benton Barracks Parole Camp on June 7, 1863, not far from the New House of Refuge where I had convalesced some eight months ago. At Benton Barracks, I was once again out-of-commission from doing my soldier's duty.

We weren't prisoners, and we weren't free, either, just in that place they called limbo. We had to have a good deal of patience, for we were prohibited from aiding the Union war effort in any way whatsoever. That was the condition of the official parole arrangement between the North and South. Once captured, you could not do any work that would free another soldier to fight the enemy. Until the Confederates had an equal number of Southern parolees in their custody to trade and release, we were to remain there and do next to nothing.

I thought it a strange and oddly civilized way for two warring armies to handle their prisoners. It made me wonder how we could make such a gentlemanly bargain off the battlefield and still kill each other at first chance on the battlefield. It was like there were rules to follow to wage war, just like in a game of checkers.

With no choice, I stayed in the barracks, biding my time. Unlike my last visit to St. Louis, I felt in good form and had some of my company boys there with me. We whittled and played cards and read any newspaper we could find. We were desperate for news. Out in the field, we never knew what was going on in the country and what the people were thinking.

By the time we were exchanged and released back to our Regiment in September, General Grant and the U.S. Army of the Tennessee had already captured Vicksburg. We had missed the fight. That long siege was finally over, and the whole of the Mississippi River belonged to the Yanks. The North celebrated, but the casualty numbers were again too horrible to consider. 35,000 soldiers, more than half the men who fought in that long effort to keep and to take Vicksburg, were killed or injured. I considered myself lucky that this time I had been spared seeing horrors such as I had seen at Pittsburg Landing.

The talk around Benton Barracks had been that General Lee was even more desperate now that Vicksburg was captured, and at the exact same time, he lost at Gettysburg. It was a bold move for the Rebels to march on to Union soil, and Meade's army was there to meet him. They fought for three days in July in that Pennsylvania town, with furious hand-to-hand combat. When it was over, they counted 50,000 Union and Southern casualties.

The loss of life weighed heavy on our President. Some months after the battle, he went to Gettysburg to dedicate a new National Military Cemetery where the war dead were buried. His kind words at their graves made the rounds through the camps and touched us deeply. He said, " . . . that this nation, under God, shall have a new birth of freedom—and that government of the people, by the people, for the people, shall not perish from the earth," and we agreed that this was what we were fighting for. We were saving the Union from perishing.

The 46th Illinois and the Army of the Tennessee were once again occupied with keeping hold of all we had captured at such a great cost. Once released from the parole barracks, us Company I boys joined our regiment in Natchez, Mississippi. On my mind was that I had but eleven months until my enlistment was satisfied. I was getting short and thinking more and more about going home to New York.

Natchez Oct 12/63
Dear Mother once more I take my pen to write a few to you once more my health is as good now as it has been since I have been in the army and not got quite 11 months to stay we are camped near to the city the pleasintes and healthiest of any in the south and would like to stay here till my time is out I had a very pleasant trip this time down the river soon as I get out of the army I think you will see me home again thare

I have just come in of picket we had a first rate time it seemed like home to go on duty once mor I hope that I never shall be a pris nor of ware again but let me fight till the ware is over

I shall not writ mutch till I here from you I want you to write soon as you get this and let me no how you get a long tell the Girls to write to as this letter is to them the same as so I wrote to them My best respects to you all direct you letter as before when I was in the regt.

Van R. Strong
Co F 46th Ill Vol
Via Cairo Ill
Natchez Miss

Camp Near Vicksburg Nov 25/63
Miss Tenn
Tuesday
Dear Sister
I now take my pen in hand to write you a few lines to let you no that I am still in the land of the living with poor health for the last two weeks I am a little better than I was I think that I shall get a long now I have just been to town today to express some money north I sent one hundred this time so you see that I am getting some [??] up a head If nothing happens when my time is out I think I shall have 400 hundred dollars ahead to start on a gain in this letter Sister I will send you and Oatis the 2 dollars you sent me when I was in St. Louis the money done me a good deal of good I am ten times Oblige for the favor I have onley ten months more to swerve then I shall be a free man once more.

We have but fore frost here this winter so you see that it hasn't been very cold here yet I shall write soon again you will get a letter from me once in to week so no more this time write soon as you get this I have not had any letter from any of you since I come south give my love to all and keep som for your self

Van R. Strong

Camp Crocker Dec 8/63
Dear Sister
    I now seat myself to write you a few lines to let you know that I am still a mong the living and in better health than it was three weeks ago
    I see Charles Mitchell yesterday he is well Dan M is in Vicks burg some 8 miles from here the last time I heard from him he had the ague Charles is well he says he will write some in my next letter home Uncle Nash Folks was well John is in California a doing he wrote that he had rather live thare than another place he had been in
    Dear sister would you like to see me this winter if I will come if you will get me a good woman I will come thare and marry before next march so if you want to see me before nex march get me a woman soon and I will come perhaps you think I am a fooling but if you think so all you have to do is to try me get me the woman you will see me before next march
    I now must close give my love to Francis Write soon

Van R. Strong

To M. Mead
Shall I come for the woman

Tennessee and Mississippi were beautiful country when there was no fighting to worry over. We had more time to write in these pleasant surroundings. There was not much action, so my thoughts turned to home and the future. I was serious when I told Mary that I wanted to marry. When I was discharged, I intended to get a wife and start farming again, and to have children, too. Children were needed on a farm. If Mary could find me a woman willing to marry me, I would go to New York and marry her just like that. That is, if we were suitable for each other.

Those of us boys who signed up at the beginning of the war were almost done with our duty. I had ten months left of my enlistment before I was a free man again. With the money I sent North, I was satisfied I could start over.

Here, in Mississippi, we had not seen any fighting in many months. The same could not be said of back east. The fighting there was fierce, and no side could yet claim victory in this war. The Mississippi River was in Union hands and the South now ran lower on provisions of all kinds. The seaports were blockaded so nothing could get in or out that way either. The Confederacy was squeezed of all life, and still they did not give in. Those Southern boys proved themselves tough fighters, even though outnumbered. Maybe it was fighting on their own soil, protecting their homes that made them like that. Maybe it was the generals who riled them up that made them do it.

What I say next might be hard to believe, but it is true. Sometimes, when we were on picket duty not far from where the Rebs were doing the same, we would call to each other, and joke and join together in a spirited song. The Rebs wanted our coffee, real coffee from coffee beans, not the brown water they made from bark and roots. They traded us any odd things they had for coffee. We did not mind the trade. We knew there was always more coffee coming in our rations. That was one thing we always had enough of. So we obliged them. The beans needed to be roasted and ground which was worth the trouble for a strong cup of coffee.

This talking and trading added to the list of questions I had about this war. It was a wonder to me that we could sing and joke together one night and kill each other the next day. In the heat of battle and to protect ourselves, we would fight like dogs, yet there was a numb sadness after we killed and watched our friends and foes die. I derived no pleasure from the deaths, except that our victory might bring the war to a close. We held little animosity for the Reb boys, themselves, who were caught up in this hell the same as us. They were not the slave owners who chose this war. Sometimes, the Rebs would surrender to us, right there on picket duty. They called over that they were surrendering so we would not shoot, then walked right to our side and turned themselves in.

As for the 46th Illinois Volunteers, we had it as good as we could at Camp Cowan on Clear Creek. We built log houses for winter, and they were fine for morale. This was pretty land down here, and the winter was mild and most pleasant. I especially appreciated the lack of snow and cold temperatures. Up North, it was cold and white a good many months of the year.

One stroke of good luck was I got to see cousin Charles Mitchell often as our regiments were still together in camp. So far, we had both escaped any injury and were feeling fit. We caught each other up on our families and played some checkers. He was a comfort and a good friend.

Camp 15th Ill Vol Inftry
Cowan's Plantation Dec 2 1863
Dear Aunt Lydia,
    In compliance with your request in your letter to Van R. I will try and write you a few lines. My health is good we are camped about 8 miles from Vicksburg in a very nice camp we have got good comfortable log houses built and are having very good times. I presume Van has kept you posted from time to time of

our waerabout and of what we have been doing so it will not be necessary for me to say much except Van and me have both been in the same Brigade ever since immediately after the battle of fort donelson about two years ago and since that time we have had good many good times and a good deal of hard times yet Dear Aunt there is a charm about a Soldiers life there is not in civil life I think of reenlisting this afternoon or to morrow Since I have been in the service I have only a furlough but I shall have one this spring I got a letter from home as late as the 20th of Nov our folks were all well Mariah is living at home Orlando that is Mariahs husband is in the 10th Minnesota at St Louis. Yesterday we had a strong tornado it blew down a good many trees in and around camp it killed one little boy that was in camp Dear Aunt I am trying to serve God and make my way from earth to heaven my trust is firm in God.

Give my love to Uncle Cousins Otis, Lydia Ann and Ada, and tell them all I should be glad to hear from them

Write soon and accept these few lines from your affectionate nephew

Chas Mitchell

To Lydia Strong

Cousin Charles Mitchell expressed it well. When the fighting was sparse and the land pretty and hospitable, our mind toward soldiering changed. My health was first rate, and I found solace in the company of my Illinois boys. Company I was like my family now, attached to each other as brothers. At this time, the army thought it wise to keep us seasoned soldiers who had volunteered at the beginning of the war. They feared losing us since we were of much better quality and character than those drunkards drafted from the streets or prisons of northern cities. And better, too, than those who were paid to enlist for another.

It was a hard time getting fresh men to fight such a bloody war, especially back East where the fighting was fierce. Enlistment numbers went unfilled and those they got were not the caliber of soldier of us early volunteers. Some of them were poor souls fresh off the boat from another country, signed into the army before they realized what happened.

It angered me that if you were drafted, and you had the means, you could buy your way out of serving your country. Trust me when I say there were plenty of low-life men who would make the bargain. These scoundrels would take the money and show up at camp, desert, and then take in more money to stand in another draftee's place. They repeated this, and the army's morale and effectiveness suffered. Sometimes they took the money and never showed up at all. They just changed their name for the next swindle. They did not care if the country was reunited. These profiteers were not fit for service or loyal to anyone or anything. We did not welcome them into our Regiment or expect much from them other than trouble.

Chapter 17

So the army came after us old-timers. They needed men who were proven, skilled, and reliable soldiers. We were tired and weary and thinking of home, yet their offer of a four-hundred-dollar bounty and a month's furlough if we reenlisted was a mighty temptation. In December 1863, Charles and I did that very thing. We decided we wanted the money and to see the war to its end. We became veteran volunteers in the Union Army, obligated for another three years or the duration of the war.

My reenlistment must have surprised mother and father and the girls as, in truth, it did me. It was not long ago I was writing letters complaining and counting the months left until my discharge. But things were peaceful here in the countryside away from the fighting. We could forget about the hard times of the battles.

In January, we got our month furlough as promised. But first there was one obligation to fill before we could head home. They shipped us up to Freeport, Illinois, to recruit new volunteers for our regiment. Like all the original regiments, we were down in numbers due to deaths from battle and disease and those gone missing. The 46th and the rest of the Illinois regiments were successful at signing up new volunteer recruits, so no state draft was needed. These volunteers were of better character than the draftees or their replacements would have been. In February, I was free to go to Perryville to see my family and to look for a wife.

I had thought of little else these months sitting in camp with not much to amuse or scare us. We were now paid more regular, so I had money in my pocket and in the bank. I could picture my future. I was never one to play the fool. I knew it depended on if we stayed clear from the heavy fighting back East. And there was another impediment to my marrying. Now that I reenlisted, whoever my woman was, she must be willing to wait awhile longer, and there was no clear way of telling how long that would be.

Yes, perhaps you think it all strange that I reenlisted and was now a veteran soldier. To make matters worse for Mother and Father, Otis had made a decision, too.

May the 8th 1864
Dear Sister
I thought that I would write you a few lines to let you know whare I am again we are stationed we are a bout 10 miles from Richmond and a short distance from petersburg we landed at City Point and then martched here I know what a battle is now we had a hard battle here yesterday we lost it is stated 1500 men but we drove them acrost the river and we burnd the rail road bridge between Richmond and Petersburg it has cut off their supplies it is probly that we have not lost half as many as reported thare was not any killed in our Regiment but some was wounded I am on guard to day but have

been relieved but will have to go on again in a few minutes I wrote home when I was in York Town I must stop writing for this time from

Otis Strong
hurrah for the Rebs
write as soon as you get this

May the 15th 1864
Father I now take my pen in hand to let you know how I get a long I don't feel very smart at present our Regiment has gone out but I was left in Camp and while I was laying here in my tent I thought I would write to you our forces are in about a mile and a half of Fort Darling I suppose we shall hear of some hard fighting up thare our Regiment had a fight the other day our Co. lost Eleven one killed one taken prisoner and the rest wounded thare was abut four thousand on our side and 5 thousand of the Rebs but we drove them and took some prisoners Anson was in the fight and come out all right. Have you sold the tobacco yet and what did you get for it how does things look around thare and how does all the folks get along have you heard from Philester since I came away from home who stays on the Vanepps farm this summer and do you know whare Vandusen is wheather he has moved
From your son

Otis Strong

August the 16th 1864
Dear Mother
I now take this opportunity to answer your kind letter that I just received this morning. Am glad to hear from you and also Mary. I feel very well at present and hope these few lines will find you the same. I could have got a furlow if I had tried very hard but I have been detailed here as a guard so I thought I had better stay here and try and come home by-and-by. Have you heard from Vance or Philister. Mother you wanted to know wheather I got them things that you sent me I received 5$ that you sent me and that I received just as I went into the hospital and the rest I have not seen we have not been paid since I left Albany and I want you to send me $ if you please and then I will try and get along till I get paid and send me some stamps as soon as you get this
from your

Son Otis Strong
Direct as before

Mother and Father were now getting letters from two sons in harm's way. In February 1864, as I was finishing up my reenlistment furlough, Otis and his neighbor friend, Anson, mustered in Company B of the 169th NY Volunteers. They must have had serious intent to join up, for Madison County was not recruiting for new soldiers. To find a regiment that needed them, they traveled

Photo 17.6 Historic marker for the May 1864 Advance on Petersburg. Otis Strong and Anson Cranson fought here. *Courtesy of the Virginia Department of Historic Resources: http://www.dhr.virginia.gov/hiway_markers.*

a hundred twenty-five miles east over by the state capital, across the Hudson River to the city of Troy. This was Rensselaer County, a name we shared.

Otis and Anson were now official soldiers in the *Troy Regiment*. They joined in spite of my tales of the brutality of war and my warnings that there was a deadly battle still ahead to capture Richmond. Maybe I looked too fit and the money I had earned gave a picture of war that was not wholly honest. I guess I presented a conflicting message. The hard times I described did not have the effect I hoped for.

And they must have figured since I reenlisted, it could not be all that hard. If they had been at Donelson or Shiloh, and seen me in the hospital and parole camp, cooler heads might have won out. I wondered, though, what I would have done given their circumstances. I figured I might have done the same as Oat.

With two sons to worry about, just like Uncle Nash Mitchell and Aunt Julia did with Charles and Daniel, I had been thinking maybe it was not such a smart idea for brothers and friends to enlist and serve together. Many wanted it that way, for army life gave promise of an adventure best shared with companions from home. This sometimes meant they died together. To lose two sons to war was as terrible a sorrow for a family as can be imagined. And some lost more than two. Some towns lost most of their young men, and at times, I feared it would happen to Plainfield.

On my own account, I felt hopeful the hard times were behind me, but I feared they were just beginning for Otis and Anson. As I had warned them, the war was raging worse than ever in the Eastern states. Those sorry new recruits of the 169th NY Vol Inf had walked into the thick of it. The South was more determined than ever to protect Richmond. And the Union Army was more determined than ever to take their capital city and sweep through the heart of the South, all the way to the Atlantic coast. Weak generals had missed too many opportunities, and the country was war weary.

So many men were dieing. President Lincoln demanded they finish the Rebels off for good, not just chase them home as had happened many times before. The President vowed to break their resolve so they would see it was hopeless and give up the fight. But he needed generals who had the will, and they had been sorely lacking in this war.

The match up for Richmond was the Army of the Potomac against the Army of Northern Virginia, our grand and brave General Grant, once again, against General Robert E. Lee. They were the best generals each side had to offer. I heard it said Lee's defeat at Gettysburg, especially the loss of all those men at Pickett's charge, showed everyone he was a tough leader who never lost his will to fight. He swore he would not allow his beloved city of Richmond, the capital of the Confederacy and in his home state of Virginia, fall into the hands of the enemy. It would be as if the Rebs over-took Washington and threw Mr. Lincoln out in the street.

Young Otis and Anson were facing the longest, hardest, and bloodiest siege of the war. And as it turned out, I wasn't done fighting either, as I had hoped.

[Morganza, LA, Aug. 1, 1864]

Camp of the 46th Ill Vol
Morganza bend Louisiana
Dear Mother
   I now seat myself to pen you a few lines to let you know that I am well my health is very good this summer have been sick but little this season we left Vicksburg the 29th of last month got here on the 30th we are camped in a very pleasant place they is from 12 to 15 thousand of our men here to keep the Rebs from crosing the river to reinforce hardee in front of sherman they are a trying to get a crost the river the best they know how they is fifteen thousand of Rebs campt out some 18 miles from here with 10 peaces of cannon they will need more that if they get a crost here for we have five batteries making from 25 to 30 cannon besides we can use the boys for brest works

Chapter 17

Mother we have had the easiest time this summer since in the army we had one hard time while out to Jackson not long since we had a small force for the Rebs but would of used up the Rebs as it was if it hadent of been for so larg a waggon trane we could of used up the Rebs as it was it took two many of the men to gard the train we had all we could do to save the traine but saved the whole all but one wagon that had one bale of cotton an would of saved that if it hadent of broke down the Rebs made three charges on the trane the last time they was satisfied by loosing one hundred men in the charge then they lost all hopes of capturing us our Co lost 2 kiled and 2 taken prisinor since exchanged

Mother I want you to write often and tell me all the news you can here of I want to here how Oats is the last I herd of him he was in the Hospital sick when you write to him tell him that I am all wright tell the Girls to write often this is to them as mutch news as so it had of been wrote to them.

I now must close by sending my love to you all write soon as you get this and except this from your Son with respects

Van R. Strong
To my Mother Lydia Strong
Morganza La Aug.1/64

Memphis Tenn Dec 4–1864
Dear Mother

I now seat myself to write you a few lines to let you no that my health is first rate and hope these few lines will find you the same and all of the rest We have been on the move long back last week we left Duvalls bluff Ark. And come here to Memphis Tenn while on our way down the white river we was fired into from the shore by the Gurila band that was secreted behind som logs wounding four of our men and 2 mules 1 horse no seris they fired 4 or 5 volis at us whare we was string close together all over the boat it was a wounder that it hadn't of killed a number the chance they had but we was soon loade and ready for them and then they had to keep their heads down or get it hurt

How long we shall stay here is more than we can tell but I don't think long as the Rebs are ninety miles east of here at Corinth commanded by Boragard it is the same General that we fought and the same place 2 years a go but I don't think he will stay thare long without some yank visiters

I have not herd any thing from Cousin Dan Mitchel for some time the last time I herd he was well Charles was in the 5th regt and that was all taken prisnors so Charles is either a prisnor of war or killed I hope he will come out all right yet they was taken in Ga and held thare as prisinors

The most of the Boys are well and in the best of spirits and ready for a fight at any time

It is very pleasant here now they was some frost last night so it was quite cool last Night but the ground hasn't frozen any yet

Mother I haven't mutch news to wright I only write this to let you know that I am well and want you to write soon as you get this and write all the news you can here of we havnt been paid for over seven months and besides that I have over ninety dollars owing to me for rings that I made since last paid it will be so I can send $2 hundred north this time

    I want you all to write soon as you get this please except the love of your

Son Van R Strong
To his Mother Lydia Strong

It seemed we moved pretty near every day, and march we did for miles on sore feet in worn out boots. Sometimes they put us on a boat to patrol Mississippi, Alabama, and Louisiana. In January, we had to get off the river steamboat in Kennerville, Louisiana. It was right in the middle of the rainy season and with such a sea of mud, one officer called it the stick-in-the-mud camp.

While we patrolled, we were preoccupied with the election for president coming up soon. The newspapers we read said many people in the Northern states were tired of war and wished it to end. Some even said just let the Southerners go and keep their slaves and their ways.

The boys of the 46th did not agree with these sentiments, and we pledged to cast our votes for Uncle Abe. It was a hard disappointment to swallow when they told us it was not to be. Most of the Union states gave their troops absentee ballots and provided official ballot boxes to put them in. Some soldiers even went home to vote with the army's blessing. Illinois had no such voting system for the election of 1864. They could not even show that basic respect to us soldiers risking our lives to save the Union.

There was a strong reason they took this stand. The Democratic Party ran the state and wanted nothing to do with helping our beloved president get reelected. They knew we would vote for him, and right they were. So they refused to pass a law to let us soldiers in the field cast our votes. They had their money on their own favored candidate, George McClellan, the do-nothing Union general who had prolonged this war with his inaction and refusals. His stalling in Virginia and Maryland added years to this war, and now they wanted him president. McClellan despised his old commander-in-chief, Lincoln, and vowed, if elected, to let the Southern states go free.

To our good fortune, fifteen Northern states did allow their soldiers and sailors to vote, and vote they did—for Old Abe! And that made all the difference in the way the election went. I hardly know a fellow who did not cast his vote for Lincoln or would have if given the chance. Or at least they were wise enough to keep contrary sentiments to themselves if they did harbor them. Lincoln was our Commander-in-Chief and our beloved leader and we needed him to see the war through to the end. You can believe it is the truth that his reelection was a relief to us all.

Photo 17.7 Title: District of Columbia. Company E, 4th U.S. Colored Infantry, at Fort Lincoln, created between 1863–66. *Courtesy of the Library of Congress, Prints and Photographs Division, Civil War Photographs [reproduction number LC-DIG-cwpb-04294].*

Luck was with me in another way. The army chose to send the 46th Illinois south instead of east. We were not anxious to go to Virginia or Georgia where the fighting was getting worse. Our orders were to move south toward Mobile. We believed the chance of much fighting there was slim. Oat, Anson, Charles, and Dan could not say the same. Their fate was to join with Grant and Sherman in the fight to the bitter end.

There was no news of any of them for months. For all I knew, but dreaded hearing, they were dead, buried on a battlefield in the Wilderness, or suffering in Andersonville, that deathbed of a Southern prison camp. There was no more parole system and trading of prisoners. Until the South agreed to treat the colored soldiers they captured the same as the white troops, Lincoln refused to parole any more Rebs. The colored troops were official U.S. Army like the rest of us, but the Confederates did not see it that way. They were just runaway slaves to them, property to be reclaimed or destroyed. They would not take them prisoner, but rather shoot them on the spot or send them back to their Southern masters. It was now enemy prison camps for all who were captured on either side. Many thought the President wrong to sacrifice white soldiers because of the colored ones.

The skies brightened when Mr. Lincoln was sworn in on the 4th of March, 1865. And things on the Eastern battlefields had started going our way thanks to Grant and Sherman, my old generals from Shiloh, true men of action and courage, unstoppable in their destruction of the South. Our regiment was taken by surprise when, one month after the inauguration, Robert E. Lee surrendered his Army of Northern Virginia to Ulysses S. Grant at Appomattox Courthouse. The constant pressure had worked, but not before both sides suffered heavy casualties.

When news of Lee's surrender reached our regiment, we could hardly believe our ears. What we had been waiting for, for these many years had finally happened. Without fanfare, just the quiet stroke of a pen, the war was over. Grant and Lee made us proud. They acted like true gentlemen and sat down together peaceably to settle the conditions of surrender.

President Lincoln was a smart man. He had planned for this day and had already started to draw up a plan for bringing the states back together and rebuilding the South. Us Yanks had seen the devastation done to the South with our own eyes and knew the job would not be easy. The land and people were worn down and poor, especially those who were unlucky enough to find themselves in Sherman's path as he killed and burned his way through Atlanta to the sea.

Lincoln vowed no revenge, and instead promised compassion and citizenship to all who swore an oath of allegiance to the United States of America. Seemed what we had always heard about Old Abe proved itself to be true. He was a kind man at heart, with great compassion and wisdom.

Again, I could not help but puzzle at the civility the generals and soldiers showed each other, and how quick our President was to bring the rebels states

---

Freedman's Village, Va., Nov.17, 1864
I must say, and I am proud to say, that I never was treated by any one with more kindness and cordiality than were shown to me by that great and good man, Abraham Lincoln, by the grace of God president of the United States for four years more. He took my little book, and with the same hand that signed the death-warrant of slavery, wrote as follows:
For Aunty Sojourner Truth
October 29, 1864
A. LINCOLN
As I was taking my leave, he arose and took my hand, and said he would be pleased to have me call again. I felt that I was in the presence of a friend, and now I thank God from the bottom of my heart that I always have advocated his cause, and have done it openly and boldly. I shall feel still more in duty bound to do so in time to come. May God assist me. (Truth, Sojourner, 1875, pp. 177-79)

Figure 17.3 Excerpt of Sojourner Truth's Nov. 17, 1864, letter describing her first meeting with Abraham Lincoln on October 29, 1864. *Courtesy of the Sojourner Truth Institute of Battle Creek: www.sojournertruth.org/Library/Speeches/Default.htm#LINCOLN.*

back in the Union. In my mind, this didn't match up with the ruthless way they had fought each other just days before. Maybe they were all as bone-tired and sick of war as we were. This war had changed my thinking in so many ways that at times I did not know where I stood on an issue or what I thought about human nature.

As you would expect, with the announcement of the end of a four-year war, our camp was filled with cheers and hurrahs and music, drinking, and good-natured roughhousing. You never saw such excitement or heard such happy talk of the future! Good things were happening in quick order, and the mood of the boys was high. We had done our job well. We had preserved these United States and were alive.

We asked our captain if we would now be going home, but the end wasn't as smooth as that. Some Rebs were still resisting, and some areas still needed securing. We learned that a stroke of a pen at Appomattox did not mean the guns would immediately go silent everywhere. We marked our time and hoped no Confederates decided to keep the fight going.

And I still hadn't heard any news of Otis and Anson and the Mitchells. Their regiments fought right up to the time of General Lee's surrender, and the death count was high for both sides. The pesky Rebels at Mobile were still putting up a fight, and the blockade-runners were still sneaking goods through to the Confederates. Back in August, the U.S. Navy did a good job of capturing Mobile Bay by boat. General Farragut was like the Grant of the sea. He lost the ironclad Tecumseh to a mine and knew there were more in those

---

Saturday, April 8, 1865

fires by the roadside. Everything is encouraging.

Sunday, April 9, 1865

Moved in good season. Marched hard. Woods on fire, filling the air full with smoke, making it disagreeable indeed. Rebs are being picked up all along. Saw & heard a man talk concerned who had lost an arm at Seven Pines, said Lee passed with about 10,000 men on that road, terribly scattered, many were deserting to their homes & said that no Virginians would fight out of their state. The woman living there had lost her husband in battle, he was buried in the dooryard, Found one reb with his family by the roadside, a deserter, who said he was surprised to see how kindly "you all are."...

Sunday, April 9, 1865 Virginia

The woman living there had lost her husband in battle, he was buried in the dooryard, Found one reb with his family by the roadside, a deserter, who said he was surprised to see how kindly "you all are."... (Patterson, William T., 1865)

Figure 17.4 Excerpt from Union soldier William T. Patterson's April 8–9, 1865, journal with observations of Confederates following General Lee's surrender. *Courtesy of University of Washington Libraries, Special Collections CVW086.*

waters threatening his ships. He yelled, "Damn the torpedoes!" and pushed through, like Grant did in Virginia. If only the lord had given us these kinds of leaders when the war began.

Over or not, it did not matter. On April 10, 1865, the 46th Illinois had another important job to do. The city of Mobile was still not ours. It was time for the army to commence a land attack. Once more, we assured each other and ourselves this would be our last fight. Hadn't Lee already surrendered and that scoundrel Jeff Davis fled Richmond? There was no more Confederate States of America!

Mobile City Apr 27/65
Dear Mother
Your kind letter has just come to hand stating you was well which is good news to me my health is first rate and has been for some time although we have had some hard times since we started on this expedition for this place you spoke about our capturing mobile but you cant say so now for we are in the city now but had some hard fighting in getting here but I don't think we will have to fight any more our troops has all left here but part of our Division and gone up the Alabama river but don't think they will have to fight any as they is not of the Rebs left to make any show the Rebs are a coming in in small squads every day and are satisfied to quit well they mint since they have killed our leader now if they dont quit our men never will take many more prisnors in a fight they sware vengance to the Rebs now if they don't quit and lay down their arms Then again on the other hand all the boys are in deep mourning for the President to think of killing our leader one of the best men living that done all he could to save the country after doing all he could then he was sold like our Savior for thirty peaces of silver but he is not dead he has gone home to heaven to live with Christ in peace whar thare is no more ware

Mother you wanted to know if we have a nuff to eat I can say yes plenty and more than we can make use of we get all the Johnny bread we want it makes me think of home when I eat it we have all the hard tack shugar coffe meat and other army rations plenty

Mother you wanted to know if I wanted you to send me the NY Tribune I thought that was the understanding if I sent Father the Chicago paper he would send the NY paper to me but if Father don't want to send the paper tell him for me to keep it I was aware in the first place the news would be old by the time it gets her but not to me for we cant get any northern papers once a month and when we do get one we have to pay 25 cts for one paper at that

I now will remind you of the forth of July is the 2 hens up a fatenning I think I shall be thare by that time

I now must close by send my best respects to Wm Sellecks Family and all inquiring Friends and keep some for you

Your Son Van R Strong

Chapter 17

To his Mother Lydia Strong
You want to know if I had herd from Uncle I had a letter from them one month ago they was all well then he has sold his farm Dan was here in the fight and so was Maries and Mary Ann husband I saw them just before the battle how they are now cant say I haven't herd but will write to them and see.

Van

After our success at Mobile, we believed our hard times were behind us. For the first time since Donelson, I was hopeful for the future. We could not let our minds think something else could possibly go wrong. All we could do was have hope.

But something did go wrong, and it was a tragedy much bigger than we could have imagined. No sooner had we shouted our hurrahs for victory than we received the news of the death of our beloved President, our Illinois son, who gave all he had to keep the country from splitting in two. Father Abraham was dead by one fatal bullet to the head. He had not even got two weeks to enjoy the relief brought by the surrender before he was murdered. The General read the announcement sent from Washington for all troops to hear, and bit-by-bit the full story of what happened in Washington traveled through the camp. We were desperate for news from up north and relied on these dispatches, rumors, and scarce newspapers.

You can believe it was a terrible blow to the boys, so much so that the camp was silent at hearing the news, free of joking, singing, and card playing for days afterward. It was a quiet of sorrow and also of anger. Low conversations were often pierced by sharp words of revenge. The anger was one of disbelief. The war was finally over after four bloody years, but the killing had not stopped there. On the brink of peace, our President had been assassinated.

The cold-blooded killer, John Wikes Booth, was not a soldier. They said his fierce loyalty to the Confederacy and hatred of our President was well-known. If he had been a soldier, he would surely have been glad to have this war over and to see peace return. But his unthinkable act rekindled the hatred between North and South. The 16th New York Calvary hunted down Booth and he would not surrender. They set fire to the barn where was hiding and a soldier shot him as he tried to escape. We gave a bitter cheer when they captured and finally hanged his murdering conspirators.

With all that happened, I still held tight to the belief that we would be discharged soon. That was unless the President's death started the fighting all over again. And what would the new president do? Would Andrew Johnson be as level-headed as our beloved Abe Lincoln?

I had not heard much from home except for the letters of my special friend who wrote me almost daily. She cheered my spirits and made me anxious to muster out. We were promised to each other, and the sooner I could get back to Perryville, the sooner we could start a life together. Mary took my letter serious in the manner I intended it. She found me a wife. Martha Hodge was as fine a woman as I could ask for, and I was thankful for my divine providence. I hoped my days as a soldier were over and all of us would soon be united for a joyous wedding. I prayed that the Lord let this war be done for good, never to happen again, and that all the boys still living, from North and South, would return home to their loving families. We had all had enough hard times to deserve some peace.

Camp Saluberty Spring La
Sept 9 1865
Dear Mother
   I have just got your kind letter dated August the 18 togeather with one from Lydia Ann it brings me mutch joy to here again after hearing that she was lost by beaing shiprect it brought many sad hour at first to here of sutch news but now them days have past and she is saived and in her own home in California and I hope she is happy for she has had a nuff of trouble in getting thare to live happy the remainder of her days and I trust she will at any way we will trust in the Lord that Geo will care for her through life Mother I herd of her luck befor I got your letter I have a Friend that writes me the news I hope it wont be mutch longer that I shall have to write I want to see her together with all of the rest but cant now for a while at least till the Gov sees fit to discharge me from the army some times the prospects looks fair to get home then again they is not mutch hopes of getting home very soon
   Mother you must have a good deal of patience as well as myself you can realize my being gone while I have the expearance it is not my good will to but have to Now let me say as you have spoke of having a plenty of corn to make the wedding cake I wish you to bake and keep one a head so that they wont be any time lost when I come please poot in some sweet apples and ponkins in it so we can have a change I like it for a change
   Mother I have onely got but one letter from any of you for three months I have wrote often but thare comes no answer the time is nearly come that I will have to stop writing if we don't get pay soon so I can buy materials to write and if you don't get any more letters from me you can ask some one els if I am well she will tell you for I write as often as one a week I hope a few more will do so I get home
   Mother we are a having a very good time I was out in the country some twelve miles from here and staid four days I had all of the Johney cake honey butter and other stuff that was good as I wanted to eat I was welcomb and asked to go back and stay a week and I am a going to except the chance for a change
   Mother my health is first rate this summer and wish I could see you and tell you all of the news I now must close by sending my Love please write often and long leters Give my love to all and except of your

Son Van R. Strong
To My Mother OX OX

The United States was preserved, but the U.S. Army did not seem to be in any hurry to discharge the 46th Illinois. At least I had my Martha waiting for me, and my dear sister Lydia was now safe in California after her near death in a shipwreck. She had George Bixby to keep care of her in that rugged land. I knew George to be decent man, a Perryville boy with a good reputation.

If only the army could find it in their heart to take pity on me and release me from my soldier's duty, Martha would soon have me there to marry and to take care of her. We would get on with our life free to live where we wanted to, make a good farm, and raise a family as we chose.

"Give my love to all enquiring friends and keep some for yourself."
Van R. Strong

Appendix A

The Rest of the Story

Main Characters

Van Rensselaer Strong
  Born: June 15, 1830, Madison County, New York
  46th IL Vol/Vet Inf Co I out of Will County, Illinois
  Hair: Black   **Height:** 5'10"   **Eyes:** Black   **Complexion:** Dark

Van was right. The army held on tight to the 46th IL Veterans. They finally mustered them out on January 20, 1866, in Baton Rouge, Louisiana, nine months after the South surrendered. He was also right about finding a woman.

He kept good his pledge to return home to Perryville and Martha Hodge. The soldiers first stopped in Camp Butler, where it had all started for Van five years earlier, and then waited five days in Freeport, Illinois, for their final pay. The regiment was formally discharged on February 1st, and Van was soon home to marry his wartime sweetheart. They likely had pumpkin apple cake to celebrate their February 18th wedding, as he had requested.

Van and Martha stayed in Perryville for some time before they went out west to Harmony, Illinois. There, Martha bore them two children. Life was still filled with hardships, though, even in a town so sweetly named. It was in the Harmony cemetery that they buried their firstborn, an infant son they had named Nelson Philester. In 1869, they took their second born son, George Lewis Strong, with them to Taylor County, Iowa. There were few white settlers in this part of Iowa at that time, and Van was one of the first to make it his home. He secured his government allotted 160 homestead acres, which he tilled and made profitable. He was finally a landowner. Iowa was excellent

Photo A.1 Portrait photo of a young Van R. and Martha Hodge Strong. *Courtesy of the Showers family collection.*

Photo A.2 Portrait of Van and Martha Strong (front) and children (l–r) Phebe, George, Lucinda, and Lydia. *Courtesy of the Showers family collection.*

farmland. His time in the army counted as his five year residency required by the Homestead Act of 1862, so he owned the land outright.

Van and Martha had eight children. Four died in childhood, including Otis and Philester, whom they named after Van's brothers. It is interesting to note his son Otis' middle name was Grant. George lived to adulthood and gave Van and Martha four grandchildren. Daughters Lydia and Phoebe together gave them five more. Lydia is Arlene Showers' grandmother, and Phoebe is Bob Campain's grandmother.

When he was fifty-two years old, Van applied for a military pension claiming a permanent disability from the chronic intestinal and other ailments he suffered during his service in the army. He submitted sworn testimony from his 46th IL tent mates, E. F. Brown and Soloman A. Shiffer, verifying his claim that he suffered from catarrh (nasal discharge), chronic gastritis, chronic diarrhea, piles, disease of the heart, rheumatism, deafness, and general disability as a result of his service in the army.

The report from the Adjutant General's Office, May 22, 1882, concurred that Van was febrile, had typhoid, and suffered from acute dysentery on and

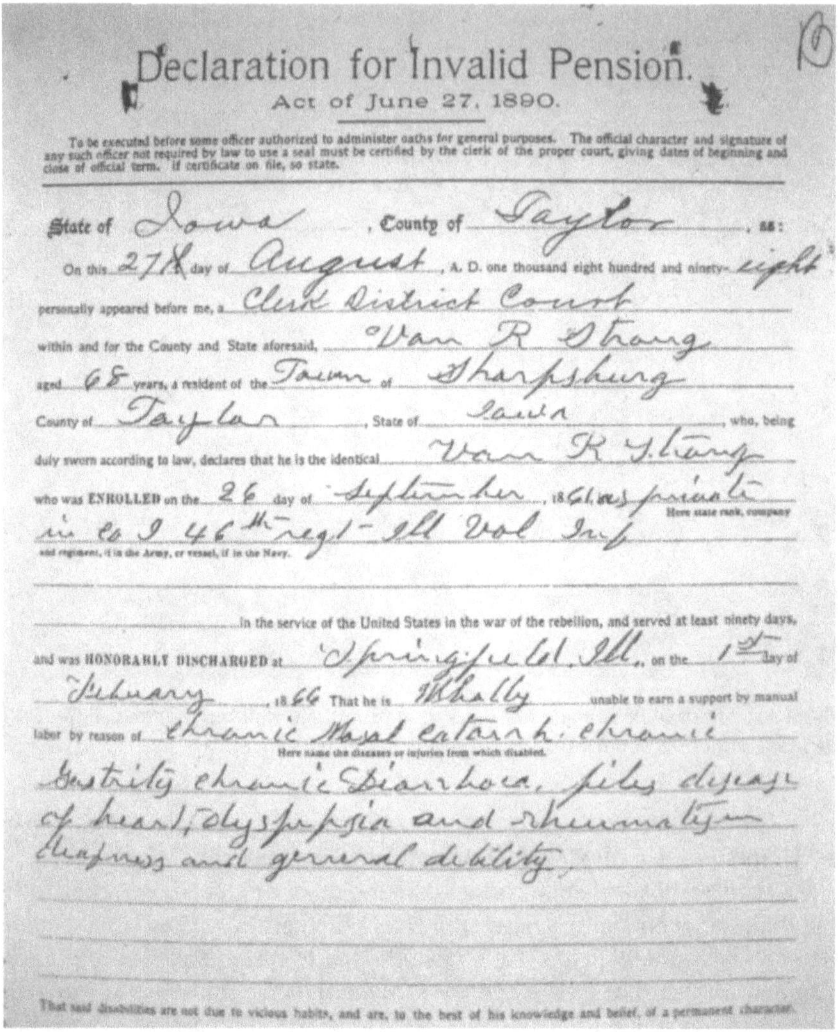

Declaration for Invalid Pension.
Act of June 27, 1890.

To be executed before some officer authorized to administer oaths for general purposes. The official character and signature of any such officer not required by law to use a seal must be certified by the clerk of the proper court, giving dates of beginning and close of official term. If certificate on file, so state.

State of Iowa, County of Taylor, ss:

On this 27th day of August, A. D. one thousand eight hundred and ninety-eight personally appeared before me, a Clerk District Court within and for the County and State aforesaid, Van R Strong aged 68 years, a resident of the Town of Sharpsburg County of Taylor, State of Iowa, who, being duly sworn according to law, declares that he is the identical Van R Strong who was ENROLLED on the 26 day of September, 1861 as private in Co I 46th regt Ill Vol Inf (Here state rank, company and regiment, if in the Army, or vessel, if in the Navy.) in the service of the United States in the war of the rebellion, and served at least ninety days, and was HONORABLY DISCHARGED at Springfield Ill, on the 1st day of February, 1866 That he is wholly unable to earn a support by manual labor by reason of chronic nasal catarrh, chronic gastrity chronic Diarrhoea, piles disease of heart, dyspepsia and rheumatism deafness and general debility. (Here name the diseases or injuries from which disabled.)

That said disabilities are not due to vicious habits, and are, to the best of his knowledge and belief, of a permanent character.

Photo A.3 Van's 1898 request for an Invalid Pension, listing the ailments he contracted during his military service. ***Courtesy of National Archives and Records Administration (NARA) Military Service Records.***

off during his military service. But they concluded there was "no evidence of disability as alleged." Records show Van renewed his efforts in 1898 with another Invalids Pension claim. Shiffer submitted a second, more convincing letter in 1893, but it might not have changed their minds. At some point, he was successful, and when he died in 1904, Martha applied for a widow's pension to collect his monthly payment.

Civil War Invalids Pensions were a contentious and frustrating issue, according to the National Archives and Records Administration's "Guide to the Records of the U.S. House of Representatives at the National Archives 1789–1989." The army's backlog of applications kept thousands of veterans from collecting money they needed to live on when, as a result of their service in the war, they became unable to work. Veterans waited years for their case to come before the panel. The citizens of Cape May, New Jersey, had had enough and decided to stand up for all Civil War veterans. In 1880, they sent this petition to Congress supporting a bill that would speed up pension claims:

> Your memorialists respectfully represent that there are now three hundred thousand unsettled claims for pension, on account of disabilities or death incurred in the service. New claims are coming forward at the rate of fifteen hundred per month. The unsettled claims have been accumulating from 1862 to the present time. There are more than sixty-five thousand claims which have been pending five years and upwards, and thirty thousand which have been pending ten years. This fact alone is conclusive of the inadequacy of the present system of laws for the sacrifices they have made for the Union. (Guide to the Records of the U.S. House of Representatives at the National Archives 1789–1989, n.d.)

By all accounts, Van was a good citizen who even held local public office. Stories passed along by his descendants tell that he was also a successful farmer and shrewd businessman, and the patriarch of the Strong family. Van R. died on June 3, 1904, and is buried in the Lexington Cemetery in Taylor County, Iowa. There is a marker next to his gravestone that tells he was a soldier in the 46th IL Vol. Infantry during the Civil War. Van lived to be seventy-four, not a bad lifespan for that time in history, especially considering what he had lived through.

Looking back on his life, he twice served under, and even stood guard for, General Ulysses S. Grant, who would later become the 18th President of the United States; he fought with Grant at the first Union victories of the war, Fort Donelson and Pittsburg Landing. He had been severely ill for half a year, spending months recovering in a military hospital, then deserted his post and was captured and brought back to his 46th Illinois two months later. He was taken prisoner at Vicksburg, exchanged, and held in a parole camp for over four months. He saw action at Jackson, Mississippi, and finally at Mobile City, Alabama. The 46th IL Vol Inf. Regiment lost 81 soldiers to battle wounds and 254 from disease, a total of 335 casualties out of approximately 1,000 men, higher than the average casualty rate.

Van reenlisted in December 1863 for an additional three years or the duration of the war. They defined the war as they pleased, for his regiment was kept in service for nine months after the war ended. Van could have played it safe and mustered out in early 1864, when his first enlistment was done. He didn't.

In his last letter of September 9, 1865, Van is particularly effusive, more so than in any preceding letter. He ends with, "Mother my health is first rate this summer and wish I could see you and tell you all the news I now must close by sending my love please write often and long letters Give my love to all and except of your son Van R. Strong To My Mother" followed by OXOX. Van seemed profoundly happy at the prospect of returning to civilian life to start over with his dear Martha and his dreams of being a farmer. We can feel the relief the soldiers must have experienced when the war was over.

And while, by best count, 625,000 men died in the course of the Civil War, he had escaped injury and survived it all. He somehow lived when over 400,000 soldiers succumbed to disease, some from the very ailments Van had contracted, a number substantially greater than that of those who died from battle wounds.

Van's descendants, the Plainfield Illinois Soldiers' Monument, Caron Stillmunkes' book of biographies, the Regimental Histories of the 46th IL, and now this book are able and pleased to honor his memory.

Van R. Strong died June 3, 1904

Photo A.4   Van R. Strong's gravestone in the Taylor County, Iowa, cemetery. After the war, Van spent the rest of his life Taylor County.   *Courtesy of Van's great-grandson, Bob Campain.*

Brother Otis Baker Strong

Born: June 27, 1844, Madison County, New York

169th NYS Vol Co B out of Troy, New York

Otis and his Perryville friend, Anson Cranson, mustered into the 169th NY Vol. Inf. on February 23, 1864. Otis was nineteen years old, and Hanson was a mere fifteen. Hanson appears to have lied about his age, as his military records have him as eighteen years old. Many soldiers too young for service lied to join the fight.

Otis fought with the Army of the James in the relentless 292-day siege of Petersburg, Virginia, brutal and prolonged fighting that saw horrific casualties on both sides. The siege was the Union's desperate all-out push to capture Richmond, the Capital of the Confederacy some twenty miles north. Remember Lincoln's telegram to Grant about the bulldog grip? The account of this plodding, tenacious, and brutal campaign is bone chilling. Bruce Catton's nonfiction treasure, *The Army of the Potomac: A Stillness at Appomattox*, chronicles this period right before Lee's surrender with accurate detail and candor. The numbers lost and maimed are nothing less than slaughter.

And while others came home missing limbs, or not at all, Otis made it through the war with just an injury to his left hand, sustained on June 30, 1864, during the siege. On that day, his regiment lost seventy men in a matter of minutes when ordered to attack the enemy. They were discovered and sustained heavy fire (Rosters of the New York Infantry Regiments during the Civil War, n.d.).

Otis survived, but his good neighbor friend, Anson B. Cranson, did not. Anson was wounded during the siege of Petersburg in the final full year of the war. He died on September 13, 1864, in the U.S. Army hospital in Hampton, Virginia. He was fifteen years old and had been a soldier for six months. Anson is buried in the small Cranson Family Cemetery in Perryville, the same family cemetery on Ingalls Corners Road where the Strong family—parents Lewis and Lydia Strong, and sister Lydia Strong Bixby—are buried.

In December 1864, Otis' regiment was sent to Wilmington, North Carolina to help capture Fort Fisher. Otis finished out his duty in North Carolina, mustering out of the army on July 19, 1865, at Raleigh. According to a July 25, 1865, *New York Times* article, after a celebration parade up New York City's famous Broadway and a fine tribute dinner, which included a special treat of peaches, pears, and watermelon, Otis and the remaining soldiers of the 169th NY took the steamer John Brooks up the Hudson River to Troy, where they had originally enlisted.

Otis had also served under two of the North's most celebrated generals, Grant and Sherman, in the most bitter of fights. The *New York Times* article heaps them with high praise, saying, "In all its fights it never yet showed a disposition to flinch, and officers and men have ever behaved in the most gallant and praiseworthy manner, earning for themselves laurels which never fade." It is typical of the accolades regiments received after the war ("The Homeward March," 1865, July 25).

Like Van and thousands of other soldiers on both sides, Otis spent time in an army hospital from his injury or illness; we don't know for sure. Unlike the thousands of soldiers who died of disease during the Civil War, he had somehow survived.

After the war, Otis returned home to the small hamlet of Perryville in Madison County. Here, he stood as a witness to Van and Martha's February 1866 wedding, following a year later with his own marriage to Martha Jane Mead on March 6, 1867. I have not been able to find evidence that Martha Jane was or was not related to Mary's husband, Francis Mead, and of course, I wonder and continue to investigate. After all, this was a very small town, so the odds are high.

Otis and Martha had a farm outside of Morrisville and welcomed two children, a daughter, Emma, born in 1870, who died at age nineteen, and Edward, born on May 20, 1884. Like his father, Edward stayed in the area and farmed for a living. Edward married Caroline Hecox and had three children. While doing field research, I by chance met one of Otis and Edward's descendants who worked in the Morrisville College Library. No one in her family had seen or even knew about the Strong brothers' Civil War letters. She was particularly excited to show the copies I gave her to Otis' great-great-grandson, the self-designated family historian. He has possession of Otis' Civil War musket.

Like his father, Edward was a farmer. He is buried in Peterboro in Madison County, a very small, historic hamlet, and home to a wealthy landowner, Gerrit Smith. Smith was an early and staunch abolitionist and member of the Secret Six who provided the financial support for John Brown's raid on Harper's Ferry. He narrowly avoided arrest as an accomplice to Brown's treasonous actions.

Smith's estate was a prominent stop on the Underground Railroad and now is stop *NY3* on the Underground Railroad Heritage Trail. Elizabeth Cady Stanton, who, alongside her good friend and fellow suffragette Susan B. Anthony, fought for over seventy years for women's right to vote, was Gerrit's first cousin and spent much time in Peterboro as well. He counted Frederick Douglass and Harriet Tubman as fellow abolitionists and close friends. I often wonder if the Strong family, the Sellecks, or the Van Epps of Perryville were aware that Peterboro, just seven miles from them, was a hotbed of radical feminist and abolitionist thinking and planning.

Otis farmed south of Peterboro in Morrisville and was a member of the Morrisville chapter of the Grand Army of the Republic (GAR), a national Union soldier veteran's group. In 1906, his sister, Mary Strong Mead, and

Photo A.5 This was once Edward Strong's farm in Peterboro, New York. *Author's collection.*

her son, Eugene Mead, bought a parcel of eighty-six acres, part of the Selleck property on Ingalls Corners Road where Otis and his brothers and sisters had grown up. Martha, Otis' wife of forty-seven years, died in 1914, and he married Eliza Mead the following year. Eliza has been added to my search to connect Martha Mead and Francis Mead.

When I uncovered the next part of his story, I was especially touched. In 1916, after he married Eliza, Otis bought the old Ingalls Corners Road family homestead from Fannie and Eugene Mead. He was finally back home, on land sandwiched between the Selleck's and Van Epps' places, right down the road from the graves of his family and good friend, Anson.

Otis died soon afterwards on January 19, 1917. He, Martha, and their daughter, Emma Strong Scott, are buried in the Morrisville Town Cemetery. His was the first Strong family gravesite I found, directed to it by Sue Greenhagen, the Morrisville town historian. As there is for Van, next to Otis' headstone is a small stone marker noting he was a Civil War veteran who served with the 169th NY Vol. Inf. He had also survived the perils of the American Civil War and lived to be a healthy seventy-two.

Otis Baker Strong Died: January 9, 1917, Morrisville, New York

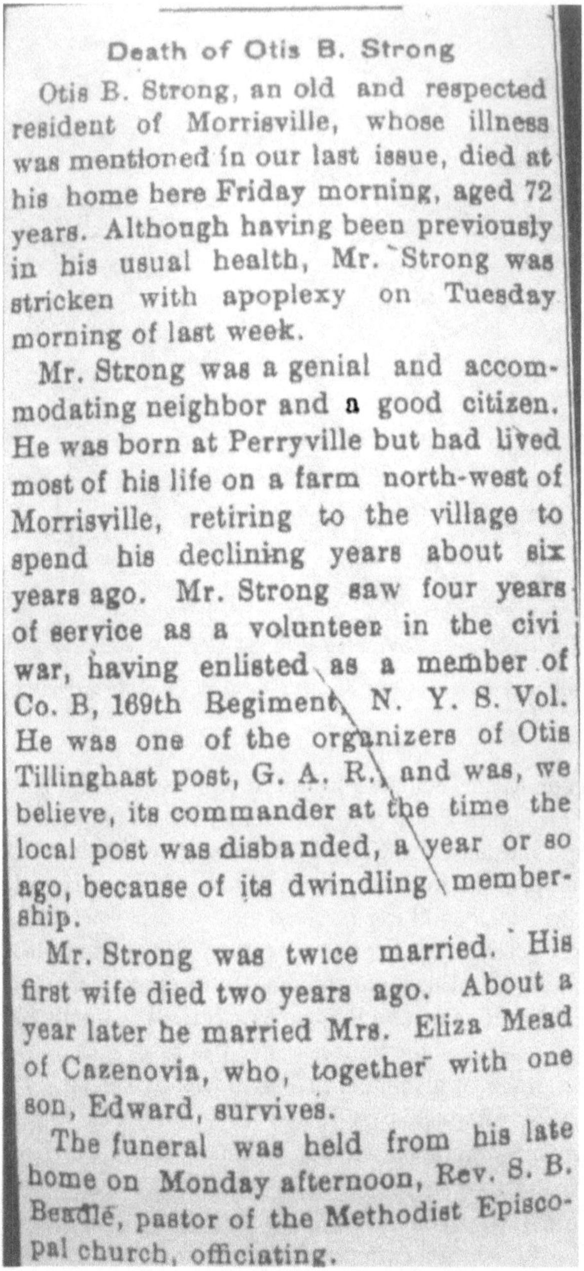

Death of Otis B. Strong

Otis B. Strong, an old and respected resident of Morrisville, whose illness was mentioned in our last issue, died at his home here Friday morning, aged 72 years. Although having been previously in his usual health, Mr. Strong was stricken with apoplexy on Tuesday morning of last week.

Mr. Strong was a genial and accommodating neighbor and a good citizen. He was born at Perryville but had lived most of his life on a farm north-west of Morrisville, retiring to the village to spend his declining years about six years ago. Mr. Strong saw four years of service as a volunteer in the civil war, having enlisted as a member of Co. B, 169th Regiment N. Y. S. Vol. He was one of the organizers of Otis Tillinghast post, G. A. R., and was, we believe, its commander at the time the local post was disbanded, a year or so ago, because of its dwindling membership.

Mr. Strong was twice married. His first wife died two years ago. About a year later he married Mrs. Eliza Mead of Cazenovia, who, together with one son, Edward, survives.

The funeral was held from his late home on Monday afternoon, Rev. S. B. Beadle, pastor of the Methodist Episcopal church, officiating.

Photo A.6 Otis Strong's Obituary published on January 25, 1917, in the *Madison Observer & Leader*. Courtesy of the Colgate University Libraries, Hamilton, New York.

Cousin Charles Wesley Mitchell
Born: February 13, 1842, Madison County, New York
5th IL Vol INF Co D out of McHenry County Illinois
Hair: Brown   **Height:** 5' 11½"   **Eyes:** Blue   **Complexion:** Fair

Thanks to the official U.S. Census records made available online at ancestry.com, we know that Charles Mitchell, son of Nash and Juliann (Julia) Mitchell, was part of the extended Strong family that by 1850 emigrated from Madison County to Illinois. The six Mitchell children, Mariah, Clarissa, Nancy, John, Charles, and Daniel, were first cousins to the Strong children. In his letters, Van often spoke of and worried about Charles and Dan and seemed to have been close with them. The Mitchell boys were born in Madison County, New York, so they had lived near each other, and then once again during the prewar years as settlers in Illinois. Yet with all my extensive research, I have not yet been able to establish how exactly they are related. Just like with the Meads, I am still actively searching for the connection.

Ten years younger, Charles enlisted the same month as Van. They reenlisted together as veterans in December 1863. From Donelson on, the 15th Illinois followed the same path as Van's regiment until mid-1864. According to Dyer's *A Compendium of the War of the Rebellion Regimental History of the 15th Illinois*, at that point, Charles parted from the 46th Illinois and went to the hornets' nest of trouble back East.

The 15th IL stood guard at various positions throughout the summer and fall of 1864. In June, they were attacked at Big Shanty, now Kennesaw, Georgia. A part of the battalion was captured and imprisoned at Andersonville, Georgia, the notorious prisoner of war camp. Van mentions that he feared Charles had been killed or taken prisoner. Remarkably, neither had happened. After Big Shanty, Charles continued on with the 15th as part of General Sherman's "March to the Sea." This ruthless and controversial campaign of destruction of the towns and farms of Georgia and South Carolina is credited with dealing a crushing blow to the Confederacy and hastening the end of the war (Dyer, 1908).

Andersonville Prison Camp in Georgia was an unforgettable atrocity, as was the Union equivalent in Elmira, NY. Rufus Bolton was another Plainfield soldier, attached to the 100th IL Vol Inf. He was captured at the Battle of Chickamauga and later died at Andersonville of scorbutus (scurvy) on November 4, 1864. This is part of the last letter he wrote home three days before his death. He actually had to dictate it to John England, a soldier in the 2nd NY Calvary, as he was too weak to write it himself. England made sure the letter made it to Rufus' parents.

The hospital fare has been and still is very poor, so much so that it is almost impossible to recover, for there is an entire absence of everything requisite to nourish and sustain life. I have had a hope that there might have been a general exchange of prisoners, at least a special exchange for the sick and wounded, but everything now seems to the contrary. (Bolton, 1864, November 4)

During the war years, out west, part of the U.S. Army was systematically and forcibly removing Native Americans from their homeland. The 15th IL was scheduled to muster out in June of 1865, but on word of an uprising of the Plains Indians in Kansas, the army kept the regiment in service until September of that year. From all reports, they were not pleased with the delay, especially when, by the time they got to Kansas, they found the emergency was over. That they weren't needed is curious, as the Plains Wars continued until 1878, when the Indians were finally declared defeated.

Charles still beat Van in the race to muster out. He was discharged from the army on September 16, 1865, at Fort Leavenworth, Kansas. It was there that Charles met Mary Ann Wade, born in Missouri in 1849. They married the following June. Before they moved back to Coral County, Illinois, they had a daughter, Ada May, born July 3, 1869. Another daughter, Mary Annette, was born on May 10, 1871, in Illinois. Ironically, as Charles was moving back to Illinois to live, Van was leaving Illinois for a new life in the wide-open farm land of Iowa. I wonder if they ever met up with each other after the war. Charles ran a wood and coal business, Mitchell, Johnson & Co. I am still trying to confirm his year of death and place of burial.

Charles W. Mitchell Died: Unknown

Cousin Daniel W. Mitchell

Born: 1844 Madison County, New York

95th IL Vol Infantry Co A out of Marengo, McHenry County, Illinois

Hair: Brown **Height:** 5' 10" **Eyes:** Blue **Complexion:** Fair

Miraculously, cousin Daniel Mitchell also made it through the war alive and intact. He had mustered into the army just shy of a year after Van and his brother Charles and served for the duration of the war. Dan suffered a head injury on May 22, 1863, at Vicksburg, one minor enough that he was able to stay in the army and continue to fight. He was in the December 15–16, 1864, Battle of Nashville and also in General Sherman's infamous March to the Sea, including Kennesaw Mountain (Big Shanty) with brother Charles, and the Battle of Atlanta. In another twist of fate, after the March to the Sea, Dan's regiment headed back to Alabama and Mississippi, where they joined Van's regiment in the campaign to capture and occupy the city of Mobile.

Daniel mustered out with his regiment at Camp Butler on August 17, 1865, listed in the official records as wounded. In 1880, he was on the U.S. Census as living in Carson City, Ormsby, Nevada. The census lists Daniel's occupation as a teamster, married to Victoria with three daughters, Ola born in 1873 in Iowa, Cora in 1875, and Edith in 1877, and one son, Daniel, in 1879, all born in Nevada. The 95th Illinois lost 84 men killed or mortally wounded and 205 to disease.

Daniel W. Mitchell Died: Unknown

The Mitchell and Strong families were lucky. They had been spared the horror of losing a son. Approximately one quarter of all of those who served in the military during the Civil War died during the war. Each of the four cousins survived their tours of duty and many treacherous battles to return home to live a civilian's life. They had beaten the odds ("Casualties and Costs of the Civil War," n.d.).

Supporting Characters

Grandfather Lemeul Strong

Born: November 10, 1767, Massachusetts

Grandmother Mary Bigelow Strong

Born: May 31, 1770, Cholchester, Connecticut

Lemuel's father, Lt. Noah Strong, was a Revolutionary War soldier, showing how concentrated all this history is. Lemuel and Mary Bigelow were married on April 26, 1796. She died eight years later when son Lewis was four years old. Lemuel Strong, in Perryville with his son, Lewis, lived to be ninety-four years old. The Strong children knew their grandfather well.

Lemeul Strong Died: March 31, 1862, Madison County, New York

Mary Bigelow Strong Died: October 22, 1804, Cholchester, New London, Connecticut

Mother Lydia Ann Bugbee

Born: July 25, 1807, Madison County, New York

Father Lewis Strong

Born: October 3, 1800, Massachusetts

Van's mother and father, Lydia Ann Bugbee and Lewis Strong, met in Madison County and were married on February 28, 1827. After the Civil War, they lived to see grandchildren born and die and to lose a grown daughter. Mother Lydia Ann was born in Perryville, New York just thirty years after the signing of the Declaration of Independence. Father Lewis Strong was born in 1800 in Massachusetts, even closer to July 4, 1776. They lived their adult lives and died in Perryville, buried together in the Cranson Family Cemetery, overlooking the beautiful valley stretching to Oneida Lake. The date of Lewis' death is in dispute. Some records and his gravestone show he died on July 4, 1869, while the 1870 U.S. Census taken at his house in Perryville on June 15, 1870, lists Lewis as alive and sixty-nine years old.

Lydia Strong Died: July 20, 1874, Perryville, NY
Lewis Strong Died: 1869 or 1870, Perryville, NY

Sister Lydia Ann Strong Bixby

Born: May 4, 1832 or 33

During the war, sister Lydia Ann left Joliet, Illinois to return to Perryville. In 1865, she became engaged to George Bixby, fifteen years her senior. George traveled 3,000 miles out west to California, and Lydia soon followed, leaving Perryville before her brother, Van, returned home from the war. Otis was discharged on July 19, 1865, and might have made it home before she left for California. As did many moving to California, Lydia made a harrowing journey by ship, sailing around Cape Horn at the southern tip of South America. For some time, they thought she was shipwrecked at sea and her family, including Van, worried for her life.

Lydia did complete her journey safely and married George in California, only to die three years later in Oregon. We have not yet found the cause of her early death at age thirty-five. Lydia is buried in the Cranson Family Cemetery near her family home, along with her father Lewis Strong, and her mother and namesake, Lydia Ann Strong. Her body was either shipped east from Oregon, or the stone is a memorial, not a grave. Either way, their gravestones still stand beyond the thickets, in the tall grass amidst the honeybees.

Lydia Ann Strong Bixby Died: January 25, 1868

Brother Nelson Philester Strong

Born: March 10, 1829, Perryville, Madison County, New York

All records indicate that oldest child Nelson Philester never did come back to Perryville to live as hoped by his family. Tracking him by U.S. Census Records, in 1840 we find him living at home in Perryville with his parents, and in 1850, when Van had just left for Wisconsin, he is listed as living with the Palmer family in town.

In 1854, Philester and his friend, George Porter, went to New York City to apply for their U.S. passports and sailed to France a week later. There, in 1856, Philester married Nancy Johnson, a native of New Jersey. Their daughter, Mary Lucinda (Linnie), was born in 1857. The family moved back

Photo A.7 Contemporary view of the bucolic Cranson Cemetery on Ingalls Corners Road in Perryville, New York. Lewis and Lydia Strong's gravestone in foreground. *Author's collection.*

to the United States in 1860, settling near Albany, New York, where they had Nelson Strong, Jr. Subsequent census records indicate Philester lived and worked as a carpenter in the Albany area until he died in 1909 at the ripe age of eighty. He is buried in the Hillside Cemetery in Essex County, New York. Van was back in the United States for the Civil War, but no record of his service has yet been found.

Pictures of Philester's gravestone, as well as those of Van, Otis, Ada, Mary, Lewis, Lydia, and daughter Lydia, are available for viewing at www.findagrave.com. *Find A Grave* is a wonderful online network of historians, history buffs, and genealogists who locate, photograph, and post pictures of gravesites on the website. The postings are for our own interests, of famous people of general interest, or to fill requests submitted by others. I am an active member of the group. I locate and photograph gravesites in my area for others and have also benefited from the free service when looking for my grandparents' graves in New York City.

Nelson Philester Strong Died: 1909 in Essex County, New York

Sister Ada(h) Philura Strong Lilly

Born: March 20, 1835, Perryville, NY

Adah also appears to have returned to New York from Illinois sometime during or right after the war. On November 25, 1868, she married Henry Lilly in Perryville and then moved to his hometown of Ashfield, Massachusetts. She died there in the early 1900s. Some of the information about Ada on ancestry.com is incorrect. They claim she was born in Ashfield, Massachusetts, when she was born in Madison County, New York. The entry was not backed by a primary source, one of the cautions we discussed when using open source genealogical sites. Ada is buried in Hill Cemetery in Ashfield, Massachusetts.

Ada Philura Strong Lilly Died: February 5, 1905, in Ashfield, Massachusetts

Sister Mary Bigelow Strong Mead

Born: April 15, 1838

On May 20, 1862, at the age of twenty-four, sister Mary married Francis F. Mead, a local harness maker. They lived in the Chittenango Falls area of Madison County until their deaths. On one of my field trips, I located their homesite using an old map of the area. It had a beautiful view and was not far from beautiful Chittenango Falls. Mary died in 1911, followed by Francis in 1912. They are buried together in the Perryville Cemetery located next to the Presbyterian Church in the center of town. In 1865, they had a son, Eugene, who lived his life as a farmer in Madison County. Eugene married Fannie Gallup, and the two are buried in Perryville Cemetery with his parents. Drake Selleck and his wife, Sophia, are also buried there.

Mary Bigelow Strong Mead Died: 1911 in Perryville, New York

Cousin John D. Mitchell

Born: circa 1838–39, Madison County, New York

John Mitchell was the oldest of the three brothers, and his February 1859 letters to his Aunt Lydia and cousin, Mary, are the earliest in the lot of Strong Family letters. John's letters to cousin Lydia Ann Strong and his Aunt Lydia Ann Strong, show he was a religious man, concerned with his salvation and the salvation of others. He seemed particularly fond of his cousin, Mary, and tells her of his long and dangerous journey by land across the continent in search of gold. John was headed for towering Pikes Peak in the Colorado Rockies (then western Kansas) during the Pikes Peak Gold Rush of 1859. After six months, he changed his course for California because "reports of the bluffs were so bad." Historical records confirm that with no direct trail to follow, it was a dangerous trip to the Pikes Peak gold mines.

In 1860, he settled in Marysville, Yuba County, in Northern California, in a land he thought was more beautiful than any other he had ever seen. At this point, his trail goes cold, which is not surprising given his common name.

John D. Mitchell Died: Unknown

One Last Letter

March 16, 1860, from John D. Mitchell to his cousin Mary Strong, written from Marysville, Yuba County, California, telling her about his trip across the country in search of gold. It is interesting to note that he signed his last name with one L.

March 16, 1860
Miss Mary Strong

Dear Cousin once more I take my pen in hand to write a few lines to you to let you know that I am still in the land of the living though separated from all my relatives my heart beats the same as ever were it a thought instead of employing my pen to convey a few thoughts to you would soon be there in your presence to speak my thoughts. It is about 11 months since I started for Pikes Peak but when we got to the bluffs the reports were so bad from there that I steered for California and after 5 months hard traveling I arrived at the land of Gold but-but I can tell you that the mountains of this state are not made of gold and it is a much scarcer article here than I expected to find it it is hard times here as well as in the states I am comfortably situated and tolerably contented and am in hopes that I shall do well here yet I trust in god and his words assures us that all things work together for good to them that love God and I know that I love him dear cousin I hope that you are still faithful to God I remember you in my prayers and hope you do the same by me we had a peaceful trip across the Plains this has been a pleasant winter I have seen but one snow storm this winter and the snow was soon melted away today has been a very rainy day and it is what is very much needed for it has been a very dry winter yesterday I saw peach trees in bloom spring is at hand and I hope to see beter times I have received but two letters from home yet it was over nine months before I herd from home I hear that father has got his house finished and I hope he may live easyer and enjoy life better than ever before you must correct all mistakes and excuse these few lines from me

your affectionate cousin
John D Mitchel

There is some question as to whether the California John adopted was nicknamed the "Golden State" because of the Gold Rush, as a reflection of the golden color of the poppy fields and mountains, or both. One thing that hasn't changed since 1860 is California's need for rain and a significant snow pack, especially near the Sierra Nevada Mountains in Northern California, where George lived. The snow received there each winter provides water for much of the rest of the state, including where I currently live.

And the story continues . . .

Appendix B

A Word about Copyright

With so many excellent sources available, it is important to mention copyright laws. Copyright laws are designed to protect the way an individual expressed him- or herself, whether through a photograph, piece of writing, visual arts, music, inventions, etc. These laws have a major impact on how and where such primary materials may be shared.

Copyright is a complicated legal realm best not interpreted casually or applied generally. Teachers and students must have the basic understanding that all material has a creator, it is not there for their taking, and they must make sure they use materials properly.

Cornell University's Copyright Information Center cautions, "Today copyright is an important and controversial topic, bearing on law, the market, the distribution of knowledge and culture, and even the significance of information in our democracy. The current economic, social, and legal landscape makes an understanding of copyright law not just widely relevant, but also challenging" (www.copyright.cornell.edu). And with electronic media, the issue is even murkier. It is better to err on the side of caution and do diligent checking before reproducing other people's materials.

Authors and others who intend to use the material in something to be published or in a commercial manner must seek and be granted formal permission to use copyrighted materials. Under the principle of "fair use," teachers have greater latitude to reproduce and distribute copyrighted materials to use with their students than do the general public or publishers.

Copying and distributing copyrighted works are permissible if they meet certain criteria such as the purpose, whether the use is for profit or not for profit, the percentage of the material copied, the type of source, and how readily available the material is. Cornell University offers a thorough checklist to help us determine if our use meets the criteria for "fair use" (www.copyright.cornell.edu/policies/docs/Fair_Use_Checklist.pdf).

Part of the challenge of writing this book was determining the primary sources that would illustrate the content and display the breadth of sources available. To do this, I first had to locate the document or image, and then investigate the "Terms of Use" policy covering that particular source. Depending on the age of the source and whether the creator is alive or dead, copyright restrictions for many old materials might have expired, and the material would then reside in the public domain.

Generally speaking, documents created and paid for by the United States government do not require permission or a use fee. As Americans, we own what our tax dollars produce, so they are available to the public. Congress passed The Freedom of Information Act in 1966 and amended it in 1976 after the Watergate scandal. The Act gives American citizens open access to government records, except those the government deems classified because of national security. Access to documents has tightened since 9/11. The National Security Archives at The George Washington University (www.gwu.edu/~nsarchiv) is an advocate of the right to see government records. They collect and publish declassified documents acquired through the Freedom of Information Act (Freedom of Information Act, 2007).

Even with such sources, you are advised to make a formal inquiry to confirm copyright. The copyright might remain with the creator and have restricted use, even though the federal government commissioned the material.

Government agencies such as the Library of Congress, National Archives and Records Administration, and the National Park Service have a wealth of source material to share. With some, copyright is unclear, and they caution that using published material is at your own risk. If on loan or part of a private collection owned by an individual or estate, use is restricted or prohibited as the owner determines and might require a fee for use, as explained below:

> National Archives and Records Administration Records Restrictions: "Most government records are in the public domain, however, some of our records may have donor, copyright, or other restrictions. Restrictions will be noted in the individual ARC descriptions. Some restrictions limit what can be reproduced without special permission. Consult reference staff for details on specific items. The National Archives and Records Administration cannot guarantee the status of specific items. Purchasers use them at their own risk." (www.archives.gov/research/arc/policies.html)

There were many primary sources I would like to have included in this book, especially photographs, that I had to abandon because the fees were prohibitive. Some copyright holders, such as the Duke University's Historic American Sheet Music collection and Eye Witness to History, charge $100, $200, and higher for one-time permission to use a photograph or other source in a published book. These are still excellent online resources for teachers and students to use! Others charged a nominal service fee or none at all to provide a print-ready image on a CD. Most everyone I asked for permission granted it to me at no cost, with blessings for a successful project.

Here are some examples of policies of particular websites:

- Cornell University's *Making of America* permission guideline states: "As per the Guidelines for Using Public Domain Text, Images, Audio, and Video Reproduced from Cornell University Library Collections, permission is not required from Cornell University Library to use items from the *Making of America* project. We do suggest that this credit line appear: Courtesy of Cornell University Library, Making of America Digital Collection" (dlxs2.library.cornell.edu/m/moa/permissions.html).
- The Cornell University Triangle Factory Fire copyright and permissions page *Use of Materials on this Site* section states, "Documents, photos, illustrations, and audio materials on this site are available for personal research and educational use. They may not be republished in any format without prior written permission from the Kheel Center." In order to use the "The Locked Door" political cartoon in this book, I needed to contact and get permission from the Kheel Center and pay a small fee for a print-ready copy of the image (www.ilr.cornell.edu/trianglefire/copy_perm.html).
- Duke University's Use and Reproduction Policy states, "The following policy applies generally to materials on Duke University Libraries web sites, unless otherwise specified on particular web pages. The materials on this web site have been made available for use in research, teaching, and private study. You may reproduce (print, make photocopies, or download) materials from this web site without prior permission for these non-commercial purposes, on the condition that you provide proper attribution of the source in all copies (see below). For other uses of materials from this web site, i.e., commercial products, publication, broadcast, mirroring, and anything else that doesn't fall under either 'fair use' or the terms of the Creative Commons license found on most pages, we require that you contact us in advance for permission to reproduce" (library.duke.edu/about/copyright.html).

As an educator, you have the freedom to reproduce copyrighted materials if they fall under the Fair Use guidelines of U.S. Copyright Law. The answers to these questions help you determine if the material falls under fair use.

1. The purpose and character of the use, including whether such use is of commercial nature or is for nonprofit, educational purposes.
2. The nature of the copyrighted work.
3. The amount and substantiality of the portion used in relation to the copyrighted work as a whole.
4. The effect of the use upon the potential market for, or value of, the copyrighted work. (www.copyright.gov United States Copyright Office)

What teachers need to do, and in turn teach students to do, is respect the concept of intellectual property, become familiar with basic principles of copyright law (for example, you may not make a photocopy of a complete book, even a short one), read the copyright, terms of use, and permissions sections of online sources, and contact the rights holder for permission. For a user-friendly resource to help you and your students understand copyright, go to the Library of Congress tutorial, "Taking the Mystery Out of Copyright" (www.loc.gov/teachers/copyrightmystery).

References and Resources

Academic freedom and the social studies teacher (n.d.). National Council for the Social Studies. Retrieved June 10, 2010, at www.socialstudies.org/positions/academicfreedom.

Adjutant General's Report (n.d.). Illinois Civil War rosters: 46th Illinois infantry regiment history. Retrieved June 15, 2010, at civilwar.ilgenweb.net/history/046.html.

Allen, Thomas (1905). Erie Canal Song: Low Bridge, Everybody Down. As cited in Erie Canal Village. Retrieved June 15, 2010, at www.eriecanalvillage.net/pages/song.html.

Black Elk (n.d.). Circle of Stories. Public Broadcasting System. Retrieved June 15, 2010, at www.pbs.org/circleofstories/educators/lesson2.html.

Bolton, Rufus (1864, October 12). Transcribed and contributed to Illinois Genealogy Trails by Lawrence B. Peet. Retrieved June 10, 2010, at www.genealogytrails.com/ill/will/stories.html#RUFUS.

Camp Life Civil War Collections: Smoking and Drinking (n.d.). Gettysburg National Military Park Museum Exhibits. Retrieved June 10, 2010, at www.nps.gov/history/museum/exhibits/gettex/living.html.

Canal Corridor Association (2009). Retrieved June 10, 2010, at www.canalcor.org.

Casualties and Costs of the Civil War (n.d.). Digital History. Retrieved June 15, 2010, at www.digitalhistory.uh.edu/historyonline/us20.cfmx.

Complete History of the 46th Illinois Veteran Volunteer Infantry (1866). Freeport, IL: Bailey & Ankeny Publisher.

Crace, John (2007, November 27). Jerome Bruner: The lesson of a story. *The Guardian*. Retrieved June 10, 2010, at www.guardian.co.uk/education/2007/mar/27/academicexperts.highereducationprofile.

Directors' Order #11B: Ensuring quality information disseminated by the National Park Service (2002, October). Retrieved June 10, 2010, at www.nps.gov/policy/DOrders/11B-final.htm.

Distinguish between primary and secondary sources (n.d.). California Board of Regents. Retrieved June 10, 2010, at:library.ucsc.edu/help/howto/distinguish-between-primary-and-secondary-sources.

Drake, Fredrick D., and Sarah Drake Brown (2003, August). A systematic approach to improve students' historical thinking. *The History Teacher*. Retrieved August 10, 2010, at www.historycooperative.org/journals/ht/3.4/drake.html.

Dresser, Horace (1859). Slavery and the slave trade. *The United States Democratic Review*. Retrieved June 10, 2010, at digital.library.cornell.edu/m/moa.

Dwyer, Devin (2010, April 28). More traumatic than 9/11? A fresh look at the Civil War 150 years later. Retrieved June 10, 2010, at abcnews.go.com.

Dyer, Frederick H. (1908). A compendium of the War of the Rebellion. Retrieved June 10, 2010, at www.civilwar.ilgenweb.net/dyers/015inf.html.

Edison, Thomas (1885, July 15). Edison Diary. U.S. Department of Interior National Park Service Thomas A. Edison National Historical Park. Retrieved June 10, 2010, at edison.rutgers.edu/NamesSearch/SingleDoc.php3?DocId=MA001.

Erickson, H. Lynn (1998). *Concept-based curriculum and instruction: Teaching beyond the facts*. Corwin Press: Thousand Oaks, CA.

Expectations of excellence: Curriculum standards for social studies—executive summary (n.d.). National Council on the Social Studies. Retrieved June 10, 2010, at www.socialstudies.org/standards/execsummary.

Fair Use Checklist. Copyright Center. Cornell University Retrieved on June 16, 2010, at www.copyright.cornell.edu/policies/docs/Fair_Use_Checklist.pdf)intended.

Freedom of Information Act (FOIA) (2007). The National Security Archive. Retrieved on June 15, 2010. at www.gwu.edu/~nsarchiv.

Government Order #140, 1862. Retrieved June 10, 2010, at the Missouri State Archives www.sos.mo.gov/archives/provost/#history.

Guide to the Records of the U.S. House of Representatives at the National Archives, 1789–1989. National Archives and Records Administration. Retrieved June 10, 2010, at www.archives.gov/legislative/guide/house/chapter-06-invalid-pensions.html.

Homestead Act of 1862. Our documents. Retrieved June 10, 2010, at www.ourdocuments.gov.

The Homeward March (1865, July 25). *New York Times*. New York State Military Museum Retrieved June 15, 2010, at dmna.state.ny.us/historic/reghist/civil/infantry/169thInf /169thInfCWN.htm.

Iowa Core (n.d.). Iowa Department of Education. Retrieved June 10, 2010 at www.corecurriculum.iowa.gov/SearchResults.aspx?M=F&CList=Social%20Studies&Glist=ALL&D=History.

Isbell, Timothy T. (2007, November 12) *Shiloh and Corinth: Sentinels of Stone*. University Press of Mississippi (as cited in civilwar.ilgenweb.net/history/046.html)

Krathwohl, David R. (2002, Autumn). A revision of Bloom's Taxonomy: An overview. In Benjamin S. Bloom, *Theory Into Practice*, p. 6. University of Chicago. Retrieved June 10, 2010, at findarticles.com/p/articles/mi_m0NQM/is_4_41/ai_94872707 /?tag=content;col1.

Lincoln, Abraham (1861, March 4). First Inaugural Address. Retrieved June 10, 2010, at www.loc.gov/exhibits/treasures/trt039.html.
Linder, Douglas (2005). The trial of John Brown. *Famous Trials.* Retrieved June 10, 2010, at www.law.umkc.edu/faculty/projects/FTrials/johnbrown/brownhome.html.
Loewen, James W. (n.d.). Introduction. *Lies My Teacher Told Me.* Retrieved June 21, 2010, at sundown.afro.illinois.edu/content.php?file=liesmyteachertoldme-comments.html.
Lonn, Ella (1998). *Desertion During the Civil War.* Lincoln: University of Nebraska Press. (Originally published 1928.)
Lougheed, Samuel D. (1862, April 20). University of Washington Libraries, Special Collections. Accession No.1611-1. Retrieved June 10, 2010, at content.lib.washington.edu/cdm4/document.php?CISOROOT=/civilwar&CISOPTR=341&REC=1.
Manvell, Jessica (2001). Hypatia of Alexandria. *Changing the Faces of Mathematics: Perspectives on Gender.* National Council of Teachers of Mathematics. pp. 15–16.
Marcus, Sarah S. (2005). New Lenox, IL. Chicago Historical Society. Retrieved June 10, 2010, at www.encyclopedia.chicagohistory.org/pages/885.html.
McCarthy, Bernice (1996). *About Learning.* Excel, Inc. p.202.
McFarlane, Arthur E. (1911, May). Fire and the skyscraper. *McClure's Magazine* 37, 5: pp. 455–482. Retrieved June 10, 2010, at books.google.com.
McPherson, James M. (2008). *Tried by War: Abraham Lincoln as Commander in Chief.* New York: Penguin Press, pp.10–11.
National Center for History in the Schools (2004). University of California Los Angeles. Retrieved June 10, 2010, at nchs.ucla.edu/standards/toc.html.
National Organization for Women (2009). 2009 National NOW Conference Resolutions. Retrieved June 10, 2010, at www.now.org/organization/conference/resolutions/2009.html#equal.
National Organization for Women (2010). NOW calls for the end to shackling of pregnant incarcerated women. *National NOW Times.* Retrieved June 10, 2010, at www.now.org/nnt/spring-2010/shackling.html.
New York State Department of Education (1996). Curriculum instruction and instructional technology: Social studies standards. Retrieved June 10, 2010, at www.emsc.nysed.gov/ciai/socst/ssrg.html.
Patterson, William T. (1865, April 9). University of Washington Libraries Civil War Letters Collection. Volume20\WP040265_ Page 96.tif , Retrieved June 10, 2010 at content.lib.washington.edu/cdm4/document.php?CISOROOT=/civilwar&CISOPTR=748&REC=1.
Primary, secondary, and tertiary sources (2006, August). University of Maryland Libraries. Retrieved June 10, 2010, at www.lib.umd.edu/guides/primary-sources.html#tertiary).
Putting historical thinking skills to work (2005). University of California at Los Angeles National Center for History in the Schools. Retrieved September 28, 2010, at http://nchs.ucla.edu/standards/thinking5-12-6.html.
Quay, James (2003, Spring). Why stories are more important than ever. California Council for the Humanities. *CCH Spring 2003 Newsletter.* Retrieved June 10, 2010, at www.calhum.org/downloads/Calhum_nwsltrsprng_2003_redo.pdf.

Rhees, William Jones (1902). The humanities of the war. Washington during war time: A series of papers showing the military, political, and social phases during 1861–1865 Official souvenir of the 36th Grand Army of the Republic national encampment: pp. 165–66. Retrieved June 10, 2010, at www.googlebooks.com.

Rosters of the New York Infantry Regiments during the Civil War. New York State Military Museum and Veterans Research Center. Retrieved June 10, 2010, at dmna.state.ny.us.

Smith, M. K. (2002). Jerome S. Bruner and the process of education. *The Encyclopedia of Informal Education*. Retrieved June 10, 2010, at www.infed.org/thinkers/bruner.htm.

Story Corps: The Conversation of a Lifeline (n.d.) Retrieved June 15, 2010, at storycorps.org.

Szasz, Ferenc M. (n.d.). Quotes about history. George Mason University History News Network. Retrieved June 10, 2010, at hnn.us/articles/1328.html.

Taking the mystery out of copyright. Library of Congress. Retrieved June 26, 2010, at www.loc.gov/teachers/copyrightmystery.

Thevenot, Brian (2010, March 26). The textbook myth. *Texas Tribune*. Retrieved June 10, 2010, at www.texastribune.org/stories/2010/mar/26/texas-textbooks-myth.

Townsend, Timothy P. (n.d.). Lincoln, Grant, and the 1864 election. Lincoln Home National Historic Site. Retrieved June 10, 2010, at www.nps.gov/liho/historyculture/lincolngrant.htm.

The Triangle Factory fire (n.d.). Kheel Center International Ladies Garment Workers Union Archives. Retrieved June 10, 2010, at www.ilr.cornell.edu/trianglefire.

Truth, Sojourner (1864). Letter, reprinted in the "Book of Life" section of the *Narrative* (1875 edition): pp.177–79. Sojourner Truth Institute of Battle Creek. Retrieved June 18, 2010, www.sojournertruth.org/Library/Speeches/Default.htm#LINCOLN.

Wass, Janice Tauer (1994). Teaching history through material culture. Illinois Periodicals Online. Retrieved June 10, 2010, at www.lib.niu.edu/1998/iht529802.html.

Weiskottenn, Daniel H. (1999). Descriptions of town of Fenner, Madison County, NY, in nineteenth-century gazetteers. Retrieved June 10, 2010, at www.rootsweb.ancestry.com/~nyccazen /Gazetteers/FenGaz.html#1860%20French.

What is a prairie? (n.d.). Environmental Education for Kids. Retrieved June 15, 2010, at www.dnr.state.wi.us/org/caer/ce/eek/nature/habitat/whatprai.htm.

Who we are (2009, April 29). What are the Humanities? Ohio Humanities Council. Retrieved June 10, 2010, at www.ohiohumanities.org/?page_id=982.

Why use primary resources? (n.d.) Library of Congress Teachers. Retrieved June 15, 2010, at www.loc.gov/teachers/usingprimarysources/whyuse.html.

Wikipedia: Identifying reliable sources (2010). Retrieved June 10, 2010, at en.wikipedia.org/wiki/Wikipedia:RS.

Woodcock, Thomas S. (2004). Traveling the Erie Canal, 1836. Retrieved June 10, 2010, at www.eyewitnesstohistory.com.

Quotes used to introduce each chapter are from "Quotes about History," History News Network at hnn.us, unless otherwise noted.

ADDITIONAL RESOURCES:

Catton, Bruce (1953). *The Army of the Potomac: A Stillness at Appomattox.* New York: Random House.

Goodwin, Doris Kearns (2005). *Team of Rivals: The Political Genius of Abraham Lincoln.* New York: Simon and Schuster.

Hicks, Robert (2005). *The Widow of the South.* New York: Warner Books.

Houston, Jeanne Wakatsuki, James D. Houston, and James A. Houston (2002). *Farewell to Manzanar* (reissue). New York: Houghton Mifflin Books for Children.

About the Author

Elizabeth Cervini Manvell has spent her career in education focused on creating a positive and productive classroom climate through compassion and energized teaching. She has a master's degree in education, certification in school and district administration, and experience as a teacher, elementary principal, and in regional staff development. Liz served as a college instructor and supervisor for student teachers, and now spends her time thinking, researching, and writing about education and following her love of history. Her first book, *Teaching Is a Privilege: Twelve Essential Understandings for Beginning Teachers*, explores the unique and critical role teachers play in the lives of children and families. Liz has two grown children of her own and enjoys life in Southern California with her husband, Arthur, and their dog and two cats.

www.ingramcontent.com/pod-product-compliance
Lightning Source LLC
Chambersburg PA
CBHW021849300426
44115CB00005B/80